Do Not Go Gentle

Do Not Go Gentle

A Memoir of Jewish Resistance in Poland, 1941–1945

Charles Gelman

Archon Books 1989

Printed in the United States of America

The paper in this publication meets the
minimum requirements of American National Standard
for Information Sciences—Permanence of Paper for
Printed Library Materials, ANSI Z39.48–1984. ∞

Library of Congress Cataloging–in–Publication Data

Gelman, Charles, 1920–
Do not go gentle : a memoir of Jewish resistance
in Poland, 1941–1945 / Charles Gelman.
p. cm.
ISBN 0–208–02230–9 (alk. paper)
1. Jews—Byelorussian S.S.R.—Kurenets—Persecutions.
2. Holocaust, Jewish (1939–1945)—Byelorussian S.S.R.—
Kurenets—Personal narratives.
3. Gelman, Charles, 1920–   4. World War,
1939–1945—Underground movements, Jewish.   5. Kurenets
(Byelorussian S.S.R.)—Ethnic Relations.   I. Title.
DS135.R93K7954   1989   89-258 CIP

To my wife Sydonie, who by the
Grace of God was spared the horror
the Nazis proved capable of.

To the memory of my father, my
mother, my sisters, and my little nephew,
who were brutally murdered by the
Nazis and their collaborators in the
year 1942, during the Holocaust.

To the memory of my comrades in
arms who perished fighting the Nazis.

To my children Phyllis and Irwin and their spouses,
whose persistent questions about this part
of the past prompted me to write this book.

To my grandchildren, Sarah, William, and
Audrey, who are my pride and joy. May their
world always be peaceful and incapable of cruelty.

Contents

Preface

This is a work of nonfiction. Everything related in it is true. All the people mentioned in it are real, as are their names, the places, where they lived, what they did, and what happened to them. Nothing has been disguised; nothing embellished.

A memoir written more than forty years after the fact will inevitably contain inaccuracies and omissions, and this book is no exception. I regret that I kept no diary. Very few people did keep diaries during that critical period, and of those kept, only a small fraction surfaced after the war. Rare indeed was the case where both the diary and its writer survived. To my sorrow I can no longer recall many of the names of people and places that I came in contact with, especially in the partisan underground. Nonetheless, I have tried to be as accurate as possible in giving names, locations, dates, and figures.

I feel I may have been inadequate in conveying to the reader the depths of terror and despair we experienced under the Germans. Even with the best of efforts it has been possible to give the reader no more than a glimpse of the terrible events of those times. To know and understand fully, you had to have lived through it.

Note on the Spelling and Pronunciation of Proper Names and Foreign Phrases

Proper names and phrases from languages normally written in Roman letters (e.g., German and Polish) have been rendered more or less as in the original. Proper names and phrases from languages normally written in other scripts (e.g., Yiddish and Russian) have been rendered in a phonetic transcription—or, rarely, replaced with an English equivalent (e.g., "Michael" for Russian "Mikhail").

In the transcription (which for Russian is a transliteration) the spelling "ch" indicates something like the sound in English "chip" and "rich" (Yiddish טש ; Russian ч); "kh" something like the non-English sound in Scots "loch" or German "ach" (Yiddish כ , ח ; Russian x); "ts" something like English "cats" (Yiddish צ ; Russian ц). The three spellings "ey," "ay," and "oy" indicate something like English "A," "I," and "boy."

Acknowledgments

I am grateful to Elsie Zimmerman, David Zucker, and my daughter, Phyllis Kukin, who were generous with their time and support. I am grateful as well to my son, Irwin, for his meticulous work on the hand-drawn map. Special thanks to Clara Koenigsberg for her valuable suggestions, guidance, enthusiasm, and encouragement, and Eric Harper for his editorial talents, and patience in typing, proofing, and help in revising the manuscript.

Part I

From Kurenits
to the Forest

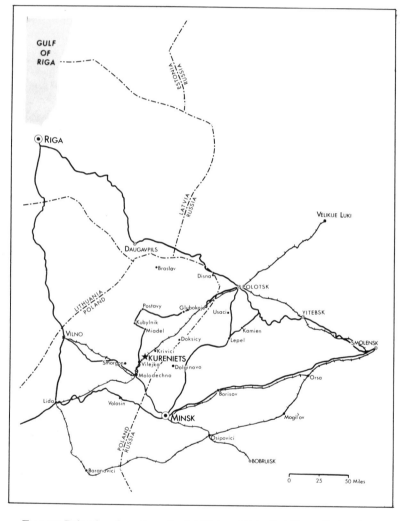

Eastern Poland and western Soviet Union. Note that Kurenits has been enlarged for easier identification, and does not represent its actual size. (Courtesy Irwin H. Gelman)

1

July 1941. We were huddling in the backyard of our neighbor, Mote-Leyb, sitting on the ground, our backs against the wall, and talking in whispers. The German army had arrived in town barely one week earlier. No specific orders or edicts against Jews had been proclaimed at this point. Yet the air was more and more permeated with fear each passing day. Even on bright days it felt as if a heavy cloud had descended on us.

Mote-Leyb's house stood next to my father's. I reached his yard by going through a hole in the back fence, as did a couple of neighbors from the other side of Mote-Leyb's house. We met there daily just to stay out of the way of the police and the Germans, to exchange the latest rumors, and to kill time. Our former routine of living had been broken, most likely forever.

That day, Leybke the barber was there and so was my friend, Nyomke Shulman. Leybke regretted not having escaped with the retreating Russians while there was still time. Not that he hadn't tried. In fact, he told us, he had made a half-hearted effort to go east. He acquired a horse and buggy, a real fancy one, a *brichke* they used to call it, and he put his wife and two children in it and drove off. They got as far as Kostenevich, a small town about seventeen kilometers from our town of Kurenits (sometimes pronounced, but never written, *Kúrnits*; in Polish *Kurzéniec*, in Russian *Kurenéts*). Leybke's wife kept begging him to return home, where things were familiar and safe. She couldn't take the hardship and uncertainty of what lay ahead along the way—air raids, hunger, trouble with bandits, just to mention a few. So they turned back. Leybke concluded his story by saying he could see he'd made a mistake in giving up so easily; he should have pressed on.

I couldn't help but agree with him—in thought only, of course. Leybke was more vulnerable than most of us because of the high standing he had had with the Soviet authorities. Being a barber and a real proletarian, his background was, from the Soviet political view, impeccable. We lived in the eastern part of Poland. When the Soviets occupied it on September 17, 1939, they promptly divided the population into politically "acceptable" and "unacceptable" segments. Anyone who didn't have his passport stamped with the designation "worker" or "peasant" could eventually expect trouble from the authorities. Because a large segment of the *shtetl* (small town) Jews made their living before 1939 buying and selling, they had been designated "businessmen." Many were just peddlers and small merchants; they earned barely enough to keep body and soul together. Nevertheless, they received the negative designation. It didn't bode well for the future.

The Soviet authorities were helped along in these and other matters by local activists who cooperated with them, often to the detriment of others—Jews as well as non-Jews—and informed on them as to their wealth, political reliability, and so forth. Some people were taxed into poverty, deprived of their houses, furniture, and all material goods. Some were even sent to Siberia as a result of the activities of these informers.

Leybke was considered an activist, although of a different kind. So far as I know, he was not an informer, but he had high-placed friends in the local hierarchy. I know for a fact that he had saved the life of my brother-in-law, Sam Spektor. Sam had been inducted into a work brigade about three months before the Germans invaded Russia on June 22, 1941. Leybke convinced the authorities that Sam was the only person capable of organizing and training a city orchestra, which the Soviets very much desired. So Sam was left behind. The Soviets mobilized quite a few men from our town of Kurenits and sent them to the German border to build fortifications. None of them ever returned and they were never heard from again.

Most of these activists had retreated along with the Soviets, well ahead of the approaching Germans, because they feared retribution from the non-Jewish population who were anti-Soviet. Some fled with their families. Others left wives and children behind, mistakenly believing that only they themselves were in danger. Many of those who fled survived the war. Of the families that activists left behind, none survived. During the first few weeks of the German occupation, such an outcome could not be foreseen. Had anybody described such a scenario as eventually coming to pass, we would have considered them deranged.

Rumors abounded: "The Russians are counterattacking." "They've taken back this or that city." "The Germans have taken Smolensk (a Russian city on the way to Moscow)." "The war can't last more than a month longer." Few of them were true. Confusion was the order of the day; for real news we were utterly in the dark. Listening to radio broadcasts was forbidden under penalty of death. News from the front was unavailable. What we did hear was mostly sketchy and unreliable.

Then, only a few days later, Leybke told us he had been summoned to the police station; he had been informed he must appear there the following day, ready to be shipped out to an unknown destination. He would be allowed to take with him only five pounds of food and clothing.

We were sitting in our usual place and discussing this latest development. Leybke said he thought the Germans would send him to a labor camp. He wasn't worried about himself, because he thought he could always survive if they allowed him to take his barbering tools with him. "Even in a labor camp, hair must be cut," he said. He was confident that he would make out all right.

Thoughts like that seemed quite plausible at that time. We had not heard of any German atrocities yet, except for two instances, which the Jewish population interpreted as unfortunate accidents.

Between the time the Russians fled Kurenits and the time the German army arrived, the town was without any real authority. It was decided to organize a sort of civil guard; gentiles and a few young Jewish men participated in order to guard against looting. The men were armed with rifles left by the Russian police and even used the local police station. Unwisely, this action continued several days after the Germans entered. Early one morning two young Jewish men, coming off duty and walking back to the police station, were confronted by German soldiers, who discovered they were Jews and arrested them. No explanation was acceptable and the young men were promptly shot. They were cousins and both had the same name—Shimon Zimmerman. One was also known as Shimon dem fishers.

The other incident involved two prominent men from Kurenits, both of them merchants and quite rich by our standards. They suffered greatly under the Soviets, who confiscated their businesses and all their merchandise and taxed them so severely—hundreds of thousands of rubles— that they lost their houses and savings and fled to another town about thirty-five kilometers away. A good thing they did, too. If they hadn't, they might well have been sent to Siberia. A couple of weeks into the German occupation these merchants started to walk back to Kurenits to try and reclaim the houses that had been theirs. They were intercepted on the road by Germans, recognized as Jews, and promptly shot.

These incidents, unfortunate as they were, were in no way recognized as a harbinger of things to come.

Leybke reported to the police station as directed and was never seen or heard from again. He was probably shot somewhere out of town. Yet such a fate, at that time, was incomprehensible because it was unbelievable. After all, the Germans are a civilized people, we thought. They might weed out the communists, but surely they would investigate with at least some semblance of orderly procedure.

Were we all naive? With the benefit of hindsight, I can say we certainly were. The truth is that up to that time we had not yet heard of any real atrocities.

Throughout the period of Russian administration there were Jews living in our town, as well as in surrounding towns, who had come from the western part of Poland, occupied by the Germans in September 1939. These Jews had managed to come to eastern Poland, even after living several months under the Germans. The stories they told were not pleasant. Jews in German-occupied territory had to wear a yellow star of David on their clothes. At times they were mistreated and demeaned, for example, by being made to wash public latrines and streets. Jews had no right to use the sidewalks; they had to walk in the middle of the street. Religious Jews in the street often had their beards cut by force, or grabbed and a handful of hair pulled out. Sometimes a German officer would order an individual Jew, or a group, to dance for him and then proceed to mercilessly beat up those who hadn't jumped high enough or who had otherwise failed to perform to his liking. There were other stories like these of Jews being humiliated and brutalized. Nonetheless, we heard nothing, not even rumors, of outright shootings.

When the Russians offered these displaced persons a chance to return to their former homes in western Poland, a large number of them said yes and signed up to be transported back to the German part of Poland, something they would not have done, we believed, had they thought conditions there to be unacceptable. Of course the Russians never intended to keep their offer; instead, they shipped these transportees east to Siberia. In so doing the Russians unintentionally saved the lives of thousands of Jews. Some died on the way from the primitive conditions of transport, which could last for several months on each leg of the journey. Others perished from the harsh conditions in remote parts of Russia. A majority, though, survived and surfaced in the West after the war.

Even much later—after fifty-four of our Kurenits Jews had been shot outside of town on the Simchas Torah holiday of 1941, after thirty-two more had been shot by two policemen in March of 1942, after news reached us of Jews being massacred in surrounding towns—people would still come up with explanations, no matter how feeble, to give the events some justification. For instance, in one town they said the Germans supposedly found a gun. In another they said the Jews hadn't filled their assigned quotas of money, furs, or other goods. In the case of the fifty-four, as these martyrs became known, the excuse was that they had been Russian activists, or families of activists, left behind. People excused the massacre of the thirty-two by saying the Germans had no direct role in it: the hapless Jews were shot by two drunken Polish policemen.

People desperately looked for excuses in order to continue believing that somehow they would survive. Married people with young children were especially prone to this syndrome, as were older people. A case of drowning men grasping for straws. The real truth of things did not crystallize and hit home for some time. In 1941, especially during the summer, we were still innocents.

After Leybke disappeared, I continued to get together with a few friends in Mote-Leyb's backyard. The news and rumors that filtered through to us were getting more and more grim every day. It was becoming clearer that the Russians were being defeated on every front and that the Germans were capturing major cities deep inside Russia— all in a matter of only a few weeks. It was discouraging.

In this connection, I especially remember the *feldsher* of our town, a man by the name of Szostakowicz. (*Feldsher* is a Russian medical title, roughly equivalent to "physician's assistant", given to a person with medical experience and the authority to treat patients, but without a regular medical degree.) One morning I met him as he was walking in the town square, holding in his hand a German grenade, the type with a long wooden handle. It had obviously been given to him by one of his high-ranking German officer friends. He was just toying with it and intended no harm. (Later on, when I was a member of the partisan underground, I had occasion to use grenades like these on the Germans, with their intended purpose.) As we met, he stopped and talked to me for a moment or two before continuing on his way. What I remember most is what he said just before he went on. "You mark my words. This German Reich will last for a thousand years." He was, of course, parroting words from a recent speech of Hitler's, but to me he conveyed the message that he completely believed what he was repeating. Then, having said his piece, he strutted away like a peacock, proud of the achievements of his newfound German friends. You can imagine what this chance meeting did to my already sagging spirits. The future looked bright to him, but to us . . . We were on the opposite ends of a seesaw; the higher he rose, the lower we sank.

How different things had been only a month earlier.

There was no war here then and, with the tight control which the Soviets exercised over news sources, we had absolutely no inkling that war between the Russians and the Germans was in the offing. (The outbreak of war came as a surprise to the Soviets, too.) Under the Russians, we Jews felt for the first time—aside from the lack of freedom and the shortages of food and material things that affected everybody—that we were full-fledged citizens, with anti-Semitism prohibited under severe penalty of the law.

I was not quite eighteen then and lived at home with my parents, Yitskhok (Iche Khatsyes), my father, and Feyge, my mother. I was the youngest of the five children. My oldest sister, Sarah, was married and lived in the town of Volozin. My youngest sister, Dina, about four years older than I, was also married and lived deep inside Russia, out of reach of the Germans. Also living at home were my two middle sisters, Ethel and Minn. Minya was in the last stages of pregnancy. Her husband, Sam Spektor, had received permission to visit his brother in the city of Kharkov in Russia two weeks before the war started. When war broke out, he couldn't get back. He remained deep inside Russia throughout the war and survived.

Our future looked bleak now. What would become of us? Minya was ready to give birth almost any day. How would she cope with a baby in times like these, and without a husband? There were many questions and no good answers.

2

One day an official order of the German commandant was posted in the public square. In both German and Polish it ordered all Jewish males between the ages of fourteen and sixty-five to assemble in the public square at two in the afternoon the next day. Failure to comply, it stated, was punishable by death.

No one knew the reason for this order, though many tried to guess. "Maybe they'll make us wash the cobblestones in the marketplace," some said. "Maybe they'll amuse themselves by making us dance for them," others suggested. Many other explanations like these were offered, which is to say, no one expected the worst. Yet failure to appear at the ordered time and place would probably be unwise because the Germans might check the people present against a list of town residents.

As it happened nothing much really did occur. About eight hundred men showed up at the appointed hour and were made to stand in the hot summer sun, facing the German *Kommandantur* (commandant's office and garrison headquarters). After about an hour had passed, German soldiers with machine guns came out of the building and took up positions facing us. They remained in that attitude for about another hour. This was the low point of the day. The Germans, with their machine guns, certainly looked menacing enough and I had second thoughts about the wisdom of having showed up. Then, after we had been standing there for more than two hours, the German commandant finally came out. He was a man about fifty years old and held the rank of major. He told us not to worry. He wished to have a *Judenrat* (council of Jews) appointed. Then and there he selected an Austrian Jew, a man by the name of Schatz, to be the *Judenrat* leader. And then he dismissed the entire group and told us to return to our homes. Except for a few cases of sunburn and of one person fainting from the heat, nothing bad had happened to anyone.

We didn't appreciate how lucky we were until a month or so later when we found out that in the town of Vileyka, only seven kilometers away, all the Jewish male population from fourteen to sixty-five years of age had also been ordered to assemble before their local commandant, at approximately the same time we were before ours. But all of them—about two thousand men—were taken away and vanished without a trace. This was followed by all kinds of rumors as to their whereabouts. Some peasant had seen them in a labor camp thirty kilometers away. Or they might be in another labor camp eighty kilometers away. Needless to say, all these reports were false. The men had in fact been shot the same day they were taken away. Their place of execution was not discovered until after the war.

Obviously, then, local commandants had discretionary power to determine the fate of the Jews within their jurisdiction. We were lucky to have gotten a commandant with a human heart. He would prove this again a little later in an incident directly involving my family.

The *Judenrat* was organized the day after the assembly in the Kurenits public square and consisted of eight to ten

Jews, with Schatz as leader. It served as the instrument through which the Germans conveyed all their orders and wishes to the Jewish population. For example, a certain number of Jews were required to go and work at Lubanye, a state-run farm not far away. Other Jews were detailed to clean the offices of the German administration, the police, the civil administration, and so on. Money, furs, jewels, Persian rugs, and paintings were to be expropriated from the Jewish population. All these orders were given to the *Judenrat*, which then apportioned them among the Jewish population. This was not always done fairly.

Towards the end of July, I was among the 150 Jewish young people between the ages of seventeen and thirty sent up to the state farm of Lubanye for three days of work in the fields. After the three days were up, we were relieved by another group of the same size. Each of us had to go work there about once every two weeks. The rest of the time we worked in or around town. Lubanye was about six kilometers away, but no transportation was provided; we had to walk there and back. Each of us brought our own food for three days with us. I remember bringing along only a loaf of bread and a bottle of milk. Food was getting scarce and little could be spared. So we supplemented the food we brought from home with cabbage and carrots from the gardens we tended. Of course we weren't entitled to do this, so we took the vegetables on the sly. Carrots posed no problem; nothing obvious was left after you pulled one or two out of the ground. All you had to do was dispose of the unedible green leafy part. Cabbages were a problem, though, because if you removed a whole head, it left an empty space that could easily be spotted. Getting caught could conceivably mean punishment by beatings or maybe worse, so I used to eat only the inside of a cabbage head, carefully leaving the outside leaves in place. Unless the plant was scrupulously examined, no one could tell that it had been tampered with. At any rate, I was never caught, and I don't recall anyone else was either.

I particularly remember one out of many jobs I had to perform in or around our town of Kurenits. During the months of August, September, and part of October 1941, the Germans operated a *Durchgangslager* (transit camp) in Kurenits—a temporary way station for Russian prisoners of war. Thousands of them were marched in on foot from the eastern front and kept in Kurenits for two or three days of rest before being driven further west. They were kept out in the open at the horse market, where, prior to the war, horse trading had taken place.

Day and night, fair weather and foul, the prisoners remained exposed to the elements. When it rained, they got soaked. As time passed and it started getting chillier, their situation quickly became desperate. Every morning a number of dead bodies had to be disposed of, a task assigned to the Jews. Fortunately, I never had to do this. In the transit camp a few of us were given the job of bringing in water in a huge barrel mounted on wheels, from a water source located outside the camp perimeter. The camp was surrounded by barbed wire and electrified wires, with armed guards in watchtowers. The prisoners were usually in bad shape, suffering from malnutrition, fatigue, and exposure. Once a day they got a watery soup and about 250 grams of moldy bread. The soup was cooked from moldy cabbage into which had been dropped a few pieces of rotting fish or meat.

The camp operated for about three months. It finally closed down at the end of October or maybe the beginning of November 1941. While it operated, at least 100,000 POWs passed through on their way to more permanent sites. We very much pitied them and, when we could, tried to help with a piece of bread, a drink of water, or a found cigarette butt. But their misery was so great that our best efforts amounted to no more than a drop in the ocean. Of course, at the time neither they nor we had any inkling of the scope of the calamity that awaited us all. Of the estimated six to eight million prisoners the Germans captured in Russia, only twenty-five percent survived. The rest were executed or died from systematic hard labor and starvation. The Jews of Europe fared even worse. They had only about a ten percent rate of survival; most of the other ninety percent died by direct execution.

During the last days of July 1941, an order came from the German authorities for all Jews to surrender any and all Persian rugs they might have in their possession. My sister Minya, who was in the last days of her pregnancy, owned one of decent quality and about two by three meters in size. She had me help her drop it off at the *Kommandantur*. The commandant saw us bring it in and, I am sure, noticed Minn's condition.

That afternoon a German soldier drove up to our house with a horse and wagon loaded with several sacks of flour and potatoes and proceeded to unload the wagon. "Courtesy of the commandant," he said. Needless to say, these food supplies were a godsend and we made them last quite a while. That major was obviously a decent man and, in the limited framework of his position, apparently tried to do as little harm as he could get away with and even to help when possible. It was always my sincerest hope that he would survive the war in good shape.

In early August 1941 my sister gave birth to a beautiful baby boy, without medical assistance. By pure chance we were fortunate enough to have staying with us for a couple of days a Jewish woman from the town of Ilya, about forty-five kilometers away, and she was of considerable help in the delivery.

This lady—whose name, I regret, I cannot recall—had an Aryan "appearance" and easily passed for gentile. Because of this she could move from town to town without too much difficulty. People with this particular endowment were considered lucky and were much envied by others considered to have the more traditional Jewish look. No doubt many owed their survival to this lucky chance. The woman was looking for her husband and her only son. They had all been in the town of Vileyka at the time all Jewish males fourteen to sixty-five were ordered to assemble in the town square, and her husband and her son vanished with the local Jews. It was through this woman that we first heard of what had occurred in Vileyka. She was on her way to some other town or village to investigate a rumor that Vileyka Jews had been seen there. She had already checked several other leads, all false. She stayed with us only a few days. Who knows how many more rumors she would subsequently investigate. Quite a few, I would venture to guess.

Two days before Simchas Torah of 1941, I was sent to the state farm at Lubanye for three days of work as part of the contingent of young people sent there periodically. It was the time of the year for potato harvesting. One of the regular non-Jewish workers, working with a team of horses, plowed a furrow about half a kilometer long to expose the potatoes. Our job was to follow and pick these potatoes and bag them. Before we finished one furrow, the next usually lay exposed, ready and waiting for us. Thus we were under constant pressure to work faster. The overseer berated and harassed us with shouts of "Keep moving, you lazy sons of bitches. You're delaying the horses." By the end of a day like that we were naturally pretty exhausted and our backs hurt from all that bending.

On our third and last day of work, the day of Simchas Torah, we were out in the fields as usual, spread four to five meters apart from each other, facing a furrow with freshly exposed potatoes. Off in the distance we noticed two people with guns approaching. As they got closer I recognized them both as two young men from our town of Kurenits and barely a year older than me. One was called Blizniuk and the other, Polevik. They were now members of the town police force and both were well known to us. I was not on unfriendly terms with either of them. As all of us workers stood facing the approaching policemen, I had an uneasy feeling in the pit of my stomach, like everyone else, I suppose. Never before had Kurenits police come up to Lubanye. The sight of them now did not bode well, especially as they were carrying guns. One was holding some sort of paper in his hand and he glanced down at it from time to time. The pair marched up the line of Jewish young people facing them and, as they went by, from time to time they called out one of our names and plucked that person out of the line. In all they pulled fourteen of us out and I was one of the fourteen.

We got only vague answers to our questions about what was happening. My mind started running at high speed, looking for some explanation of why I had been selected to be arrested. I had certainly been no activist for the Russians; in fact, during the almost two years of their administration, I had come to dislike their system. It must be, I thought, that my name had somehow got mixed up with the name of a distant relative of mine, with the same family name, who *was* an activist. Yes, that must be it, I thought. I'd be able to straighten this out once we got to the police station. A feeling of hope and belief in some order—a feeling that the world wasn't totally upside down—still prevailed then.

It was about six kilometers from Lubanye to Kurenits. The first five kilometers were through woods and the last, just before Kurenits, was through open fields. In the woods we walked together with the policemen, mingling and talking like old friends. One of our group of fourteen was a young man by the name of Arke Ruvke's, Aaron the son of Ruvke. He was about three years older than I and quite strong physically. Halfway through the woods something happened that shook me to the core. Arke walked alongside of me for a while and whispered, "They're going to kill us. Let's overwhelm them now before we get out of the woods." Properly organized, this could probably have been accomplished easily. But the idea seemed preposterous. Why should these people want to kill us? I considered myself innocent of any wrongdoing and so did everyone else in the group. And what would happen after the pair was overwhelmed? Where would we go then? We would be fugitives and unable to move freely. And what about our families? They might all be punished, even shot. Much later, by the way, after we had become less naive and the true nature of what the Germans intended became clearer, that uncertainty about what could happen to their families kept most people in check and restrained them from running away to the woods or giving more open expression of revolt. Needless to say, I disregarded Arke's suggestion and so did others he also tried to persuade.

What really impressed me at the time, though, was the look in his eyes. It took me back to my schooling under the Soviets, where I had to read quite a few of the Russian classics. In one story, by Lermontov, a young nobleman in the military is assigned, because of some infraction of discipline, to an out-of-the-way garrison where there are no young women. The boredom is great. When the commander's daughter comes to visit, the young nobleman promptly falls in love with her, as do several other officers, and one of them challenges the young nobleman to a duel over the young woman. A friend of the nobleman's, in the course of preparations for the duel, foretells that the nobleman will die in the coming encounter. When asked how he can know an outcome before it happens, he answers that the eyes of a man who is about to die reflect death for an hour or two before the event and that this can be seen by anyone who looks into them. The nobleman fights the duel and, of course, is killed.

The story made quite an impression on me. I remember wondering whether that was really possible. Now, looking into Arke's eyes as he talked to me about overwhelming the policemen, I was sure I saw death. I remember thinking clearly, "Oh my God, if he is just about to die, then the fate of the rest of us is also sealed. Can this really be?" The mind will not accept such a verdict willingly or easily— not on such short notice and especially not if known to be based on a work of romantic fiction.

We all continued walking together toward Kurenits, still in a more or less friendly atmosphere. I began feeling more nervous from the moment I saw Arke's eyes and I now considered the chances of a satisfactory ending to this episode greatly reduced. Where were they taking us? And what actually lay in wait for us when we got there? The answers to these questions were not long in coming.

As soon as we came out of the woods into the open country, the policemen's demeanor changed abruptly. They fell back about three meters behind us and pointed their rifles at us. Gone was their former amiable and comradely behavior. We now had behind us two snarling policemen ready to shoot at the slightest provocation. They began and kept up a diatribe accusing us Jews of helping the Soviets, and spat out a story about how a man called Peter—one of their unofficial leaders, who had been arrested by the Soviets shortly before the war started—had been executed in the jail in Vileyka.

This last was probably true. We had heard rumors that the Russian security forces executed all their prisoners in that jail, and most likely in all the other jails under their control, because there was not enough time to evacuate them. After the Russians left and before the Germans arrived, relatives and friends of prisoners rushed to the jail and discovered the remains of their loved ones, all executed. It was easy to imagine the anger and rage of the two policemen at such atrocities, but why pick on us? Peter was young and well liked in the Jewish community. He mixed with Jewish men his age in friendly fashion and was definitely no Jew-hater. His arrest had nothing to do with Jews, his execution even less. Both were the result of a brutal political system that victimized Jew and non-Jew alike. But all of this was of no interest to the two policemen. It became more and more clear that what motivated them was a need for revenge—not for something we had done, but for something the Soviets had done. Throughout history Jews have been scapegoats for people who wanted to vent their anger at a higher authority beyond their reach, an authority at whom they could only grit their teeth. What a convenient punching bag the Jews made under the Germans. No one was punished for injuring or even killing a Jew. Little did I suspect at this time that one of these two policemen, together with yet another, would a few months later in March 1942, go on a rampage and kill thirty-two Jews in Kurenits, my father and two of my sisters among them. And for this the pair were not punished at all, but actually praised by the Germans. I was told that an article appeared in a White Russian newspaper printed in the German-occupied city of Minsk, the capital of White Russia, describing the pair as great patriots of White Russia.

We were well out of the woods now with only open space between us and the first houses of the town. As we got closer, we came upon some armed German soldiers, which was very odd because there weren't supposed to be any Germans in town. There were none when we left for Lubanye two days earlier. The German major and his company of troops had been in charge for just the first five or six weeks of the German occupation. When they left, the town came under civilian administration and there had been no Germans in town since then.

The German soldiers let us pass. At close range their uniforms and insignia looked different. They were, as we found out later, SS *Einsatzkommandos* (SS Emergency

Strike Force), who specialized in exterminating supposed enemies of the German Reich within conquered territories—communists, Jews, gypsies, and others. (SS stood for *Schutzstaffel*, or "Protection Detachment," an elite guard also known as the "Black Shirts.") We were going by houses now. A little farther on was the house of a schoolmate of mine, a young woman whose name was Khayke Rabunski. As we walked by, I saw her standing at a window, looking out. When she saw us being led by policemen, she threw her hands together in an exclamation of horror and I distinctly heard her cry out, "Oh, dear God, they're taking Khaskl away." (Khaskl is my Jewish name.)

It soon became apparent something horrible was happening in Kurenits. The street we were being marched down led to the public square in the center of town. We were coming to a small bridge over a stream, and right next to this bridge stood Arke's house. As we marched past, Arke suddenly bolted into his yard and sprinted on through into the open fields, with one of the policemen in hot pursuit. The other policeman ordered the rest of us to start running and hit me in the back with his rifle butt by way of encouragement. We were driven at a fast trot over the remaining half kilometer to the police station in the town square.

Before we were herded into the police station, we saw a group of about twenty-five Jews, mostly women and children, standing under guard in front. Once inside, we were locked up in a small room. Two Kurenits Jews who had been put there before us were sitting on the floor in a corner. One was a childhood friend of mine and a classmate, Nokhum Alperovits, and the other was Velvl Rabunski. "What's going on here?" The question seemed to come from everybody at once. "They're going to kill us. That's what's going on," they answered and proceeded to tell us how they had been arrested the night before. One group, they said, had already been taken outside of town, made to dig their own graves, and had then been shot. "They'll be coming for the rest of us soon."

Velvl Rabunski's wife, Rosa, worked as a maid at the police station. Thanks to her intervention and pleading, Velvl had been allowed to stay behind temporarily. Nokhum had been picked up too late to be sent out with the first party. They said they had no hope whatever of getting out of this alive. I remember proposing that when we were taken out we should all run in different directions so that one or two might survive. The response I got was, "What's the use? They'll get us anyway." I had to admit the chances of success were really slim. And so we too sank to the floor ready for the worst. We too lost all hope.

We arrived at the police station about noon. We would stay there until five or so in the afternoon. All that time we expected that the door would open at any moment and that we would be led away by the Germans and shot. When the door finally did open, the person who came in was Matros, the former principal of the public high school where Nokhum and I had both been students. He was a major in the Polish army reserves and a recognized leader in the local Polish community. Matros later paid for this honor with his life, along with his wife and one of their two grown sons, late in the spring of 1942, when the Germans liquidated the Polish leadership and intelligentsia. There were rumors that the other son, who at the time lived with a relative in another town, later became a German collaborator. The principal spoke to us encouragingly and when he left we felt at least a glimmer of hope returning.

About an hour later, we were all released. To this day I'm not sure why we were let go. The principal, I realized later, wasn't influential enough to accomplish our release on his own. There were rumors that the Germans, after taking the second group (the one we saw standing in front of the police station when we came in) and disposing of them in the same manner as the first, were too lazy to take out still another group, especially so late in the afternoon. Maybe they had another job scheduled somewhere else the next day. In any case, by then they had disappeared from Kurenits. For a period of several hours we had been without any hope at all. I remember Velvl Rabunski saying at one point, "What a beautiful world this will be after the war. Hitler is definitely going to be defeated"—in this we all concurred—"but we aren't going to be around to see him defeated or to enjoy life afterwards. Because we're all going to be dead in a few hours." No one contradicted him. It certainly looked true enough at the moment. I was barely eighteen; at such a tender age it is quite terrible to expect life to end in a short hour or two. But miracles do happen and here I was, back with my family, free of the nightmare.

By the next morning it was possible to take stock of the terrible events of the previous thirty-six hours: in all, the SS had killed fifty-three Jews, over half of them women and children. Some of those picked up were the families of the activists who had fled eastward. Some were young men who never cooperated with the Soviets except by holding a regular job. They went to their deaths with their families—parents, sisters, and brothers. They were forced to dig their own mass grave and were then shot.

Two young men—one, about twenty years old, the younger son of Pinye the kosher butcher and the other, Osher from Dolhinov Street, about thirty years old—managed to break away from the pit and run back toward town with Germans and police in pursuit. They made it to a barn on Dolhinov Street and tried to hide there, but were discovered, beaten severely, and then dragged back to the pit and shot.

I was very anxious to find out what had happened to Arke, one of the fourteen in our group brought back from Lubanye, who had run away. The news was not long in coming. According to witnesses who saw and heard everything, the policeman giving chase to Arke caught up with him, whereupon Arke turned around and grabbed the policeman's rifle. Being of superior strength he was able to wrestle it away from the policeman. This was more the result of inspiration of the moment than calculation because as soon as Arke found himself in possession of the gun, he realized that he didn't know what to do with it. As I explained previously, we weren't yet psychologically ready to oppose the authorities actively, much less grab a gun and shoot a German or a policeman and then escape into the woods. The policeman sensed Arke's state of mind and took advantage of it. In a honeyed voice he said, "Oh, come on, Arke. Stop fooling around. Give me the gun and we'll walk back." Arke hesitated, his fate hanging in the balance as seconds slid by. Then, spurred by his desperate will to survive, Arke made a final attempt to escape. After heroically wrestling the gun away from the policeman, he had some measure of hope and encouragement.

With the gun in his hands he took off at high speed heading towards the village of Pukien and the woods beyond it. But his act of desperation was like jumping from the fire into the frying pan. The chances of making his escape were practically nil. The town was surrounded by police and SS troops. Arke was running in an open field and made quite a visible target. Shots were fired at him from several directions and before Arke covered the first thirty meters he was brought down by a bullet. He crumpled to the ground unable to move. Several policemen surrounded him. Then Blizniuk, the first policeman who chased Arke from the moment he broke away from our group closed in, retrieved his gun and shot Arke dead at close range as he lay wounded on the ground. He became the fifty-fourth victim.

My father compiled a detailed list of all fifty-four of the victims, including their first and last names, their ages, their addresses, and the names of their parents. The list was found in his suit pocket after he himself was killed, about six months later, by this same Blizniuk.

It was a miracle I had not succumbed along with the fifty-four. What we needed in those times was something on the order of a new miracle every day. The great majority of the Jews didn't get the benefit of even one; a few were saved miraculously not once but several times over, only to run out of miracles after successfully dodging death these three or four more times. However, there were no miracles for Arke that day. I believe he somehow sensed that his end was at hand, and even though he tried desperately to avoid it, his growing agitation brought the inevitable to pass.

3

Before the war, Vileyka was an unpretentious, middle-sized town of about 15,000 inhabitants, 4,000 of whom were Jews. Late in October 1941 it became the seat of the provincial government. Actually the Soviets had earlier raised Vileyka to this high status by making it the capital of what was once called *Vilner gubernie* (Vilno province). The city of Vilno (Polish *Wilna* Lithuanian *Vilnius*) had always been the capital of Lithuania, except for the period between the two world wars, when it was annexed to Poland. In October 1939 the Russians generously returned Vilno to Lithuania, along with a few neighboring towns, and Vilno once more became the capital—only to be annexed by the same Russians a few months later, along with the rest of the country, and made one of the Soviet republics as it still is today.

The Germans cut Vileyka province in two. Gluboke was made the capital of the northern half, while the city of Vileyka was retained as the capital of the southern half. The provincial governor—called *Gebietskommissar*—along with scores of officials, both military and civilian, took up residence in Vileyka. Dozens of German businessmen also settled there in order to appropriate as much grain, cattle, and clothing as possible from our province for the German population back home. The military did their own separate requisitioning. All these people, with their staffs and secretariats, constituted quite a sizable number of Germans in need of living quarters and office space.

All that was left of the Jewish population of Vileyka at this time were women, children, and a few old men. All the men between the ages of fourteen and sixty-five had been executed at the beginning of the German occupation. Many of the houses and offices of Jews were empty and abandoned; some had been partially destroyed by looters. The Germans needed these living quarters and office space restored quickly for their own use. They ordered a number of carpenters, cabinetmakers, and painters to be sent from Kurenits to work in Vileyka. I joined the ranks of the painters.

Painting came naturally to me even though most of what I knew about it came only from watching painters working. As a child I loved to watch people at work, any kind of work. I could stand for hours watching, with equal fascination, blacksmiths, shoemakers, tailors, carpenters, painters, and all the other artisans as they practiced their trades. My brother-in-law, Sam Spektor, was a trained artist-painter and produced beautiful canvases, undoubtedly the kind of work he loved best. However, to make a living in those days, he had to devote some of his time to other, less artistic work, like painting houses. I had the opportunity to watch him at work more than anyone else and I picked up enough about painting houses to be able to pass as an experienced housepainter.

It was becoming clearer that working people who could make themselves useful to the Germans stood a better chance of survival. If work was required, then so were workers. And the more important the job, the better was this chance. Suddenly everybody wanted to work, especially if they could get an official certificate indicating their new job status. A work certificate was very desirable and became a much sought-after talisman, as if this alone could make the difference between life and death. Many paid a high price, even gold, to obtain one. A few unscrupulous people, helped by some officials and even some Germans, made a thriving business out of selling work certificates. But in the end most of these certificates proved of little value. Only a few of the most highly skilled workers—those the Germans really needed and could not do without—were spared, but only for a while.

I became one of the painters working for the *Gebietskommissar* in Vileyka. Because his was the highest provincial authority, working for him gave us a greater sense of protection. This proved valuable when the Germans decided later on to finish off what remained of the Vileyka Jews. I was one of the five painters from Kurenits: two adults, Yosef Zuckerman (Yosef Saras) and Irma Meir-Aarons, and three young male apprentices, Hershl Zimmerman (Hershl der Krivitser), his brother Judl, and I. We worked six days a week. Saturday afternoons we were allowed to go home to Kurenits, stay there overnight and part of Sunday, and then return to Vileyka Sunday afternoon. We were not paid, nor were we supplied with any food. We had to bring with us food enough to last the week.

There wasn't much I could take with me, since food reserves at home were meager and dwindling. But there was bread enough to eat. Sometimes in the evening, after work, we used to cook a soup of barley, beans, or such. Once in a while we obtained milk. And that was pretty much our constant daily fare. Such delicacies as meat, butter, and eggs were seen only in dreams. Breakfast consisted of bread and hot water. I called it "tea with buttered bread (*broyt mit puter mit tey*)" because that was what I used to have for breakfast at home before the war. So what if there was no butter to put on the bread and no tea or sugar to go with the hot water. I made believe it was the same old "tea with buttered bread." Once I got used to it, it wasn't so bad really, especially since I knew that some people had it much worse.

The first few weeks we painters were in Vileyka we slept on the floor of whatever house we were working in. These houses were unoccupied at the time and the Germans would not move in until all the work was completed and the houses thoroughly cleaned. After four or five weeks of this sleeping about, we were placed in a house where an old Jewish woman lived by herself. She had lost her husband and two sons in August when the Germans took all the men away. It was arranged for a young woman from Kurenits to be our cook and prepare some dishes for us from the few supplies available. She was Nokhum Alperovits's middle sister, Henia. The house was small and had only a kitchen, a bedroom, and a living room. Henia slept in the bedroom with the old woman, while the five of us painters slept in the living room, the older men on the two couches, one person on the table, and the other two on the floor. It was crowded and not easy to get a good night's sleep.

One day I met a young man a few years older than I who was a native of Vileyka and one of only a handful of younger Jewish men still alive in Vileyka. This young man invited me to sleep in his house, where there was a sofa I could use. I accepted gladly. For about two months I spent my evenings and stayed overnight with his family, which included his father, about seventy-five years old, and his older sister, about forty. Her husband had been taken away with the other men in July. They were nice people and I felt quite at home with them. Food was scarce, so I never ate with the family at their house. I had my supper, or what passed for supper, at the house where the other painters stayed.

One of our first jobs was to paint the inside of a house that was to be used by the *Gebietskommissar*. The Germans supplied the paint and other materials. How important the job was and how quickly it had to be done was underlined when the civil administration of Vileyka sent over some non-Jewish painters to lend us a hand. These men were paid a full wage in money and got extra food rations and cigarettes. This was the only time we ever worked on any job with non-Jews. As it turned out we had to repeat this particular job several times over before receiving the *Gebietskommissar*'s nod of approval. Only after the third or fourth painting was he finally satisfied and then he gave us each a pack of cigarettes. Cigarettes were the unofficial currency of the time and could be traded for food or other essentials. I used to bring mine home to my father, who craved cigarettes. Smoking was more important than food for him.

After the governor's house was finished, we had to paint the houses and offices of lesser officials. We also worked on repainting their theater. What I remember most, however, was working on the house of the chief of the local SD, which stands for *Sicherheitsdienst* (Security Service). The SD were part of the SS and their sole mission was exterminating Jews and gypsies and all others they considered undesirable. The number of Germans in these local SD units was not great—perhaps about thirty in all—but in less than two years they were responsible for exterminating about eighty-five percent of all the Jews in the province under their jurisdiction. Only a few Jews managed to survive through 1943 and into 1944. Other provinces had similar SD units who also proved themselves equal to their assigned mission.

The Germans couldn't accomplish this all by themselves. It wouldn't have been physically possible. They were assisted by special volunteers recruited in Latvia, Lithuania, and the Ukraine—countries known for their widespread anti-Semitism. These volunteers were part of the SD units and wore the same uniforms as the Germans did, with the same skull insignia on their hats. They were zealous and efficient and did most of the actual killing, while the Germans took on more of a supervisory role. It was a labor of love for these volunteers, who all seemed to be selected for size: they stood at least two meters tall or more and weighed at least 100 kilos. Their imposing presence and the wild look in their eyes instilled fear in our hearts and mesmerized us as effectively as a cobra mesmerizes its prey.

The house of the SD chief formerly belonged to the warden of the big jailhouse in Vileyka under the Polish administration. Later the warden's house was taken over by the Russians and then by the chief of the SD. It stood next to the courthouse, in the same compound, on a hill overlooking the jail. Both buildings were of impressive size. The former courthouse was used by the SD for offices, interrogation, and torture.

It took us about three weeks to complete the paint job to the SD chief's satisfaction. During the time we were working on the house, he came by a couple of times to check on how the work was progressing. You could not imagine a more soft-spoken, amiable man. We were, nonetheless, under no illusions about what cruelty the man was capable of. The distinctive smell of burning human flesh assaulted our nostrils most of the time we were working on the chief's house. Relief came only when the prevailing winds shifted for a while. Dozens of human beings were being shot in Vileyka every day, then thrown into a huge pit near the old courthouse and burned. The fire in the pit was fed by a constant flow of gasoline or kerosene and it burned day and night for as long as the SD was there, that is, approximately three years. People were continually brought into the old courthouse to be interrogated, tortured, and incarcerated. Sooner or later most of them wound up in the pit, where they were converted into reeking particles that permeated the air for blocks around.

Anyone approaching the SD compound within a wide area was assaulted by the stench of carbonized human bodies.

During the time we worked there, around Christmas of 1941, the victims were mostly non-Jews: gypsies, communists or people suspected of being in sympathy with the Soviets, and intellectuals considered unreliable, especially if they were Polish and in the Polish leadership. Several months later, the former principal of the Kurenits public school, Matros, was brought in along with his wife and grown son. They ended up in the pit. There were undoubtedly some Jewish victims too, but I knew of only one such family.

Late one afternoon, after work, when I came into the house where I was staying temporarily, I found a frightened little girl of about ten sitting at the table. There was caked blood behind her left ear, her eyes were glazed and showed signs of shock and stress, and her speech was semi-coherent. She'd already told the family with whom I was staying the story of what had happened to her and her family.

Her parents and the three children, of which she was the youngest, lived in the village of Neyka, about nine kilometers east of Kurenits. Their family was one of only three still living there; most Jews had abandoned village life and moved into the larger towns after the first world war. But there were still a few holdouts. The girl's family decided to move into Kurenits to be near other Jews during these difficult times. They may also have had relatives there. They were on the road, coming in by horse and wagon, when they were arrested. Jews had no right to move from one place to another without specific authorization. Jews also had no right to use a horse and wagon. Actually they had no right to anything. If caught on a road traveling, they were especially fair game. It was not clear whether the girl's family was intercepted by chance or whether they were denounced by their former neighbors. They wound up in the SD compound in Vileyka.

A visit to the SD compound was a one-way trip. There should have been a sign on the gates of the compound with these words, to reflect its true function: "Through these gates people enter but never leave." The girl's whole family was shot. Sometimes bodies weren't thrown into the burning pit right away, and that's what happened in this case. Fortunately, the bullet did no more than graze the girl's skull behind the left ear and leave her stunned. We could only guess how long she had remained in that state. It may have been minutes, or it may have been an hour or two. When she did come to, she crawled to a hole in the fence around the compound and escaped. She wandered around in shock for a while and then knocked on the door of a house, of non-Jews as it turned out. By chance, good people lived there and they brought her over to our house. We calmed her down as best we could and she stayed the night with us. The next day she was somehow smuggled into Kurenits, where she must have shared the eventual fate of most Kurenits Jews; I don't believe she survived.

After two months we decided that because of the strict night curfew it would be best for me to come back and stay overnight with the other painters. So I gave up the more comfortable lodging I had enjoyed with the family and moved back with my co-workers.

Later we heard that the old man of the family had been arrested one evening and was being held in the jail. A strict curfew was in force from sundown to sunup. At night all windows had to be covered so that no light could show through. The old man's house had wooden shutters that effectively blocked the light their kerosene lamp gave off. It so happened, however, that a knot in the shutter wood shrank just enough to become loose and fall out. This left a hole the size of a quarter which nobody in the family noticed. Unfortunately, one evening the police or the SD passed by and saw the tiny ray of light coming through the shutter. They arrested the old man. His young son who had befriended me recognized what the nighttime knock at the door might be and managed to hide successfully.

I saw the old man once more, and I wish I had not, because whenever I think of him and his family, this last scene comes back before my eyes. One afternoon, while I was coming back from work, I saw the old man and another inmate from the jail, under guard, digging and pushing a stalled German car out of a snowbank. The old man's face was marked with welts and cuts; one eye was swollen shut. He was obviously being beaten and tortured. Maybe this was the last time he was outside of that jail. Just when he actually perished I do not know, but neither he nor his son nor his daughter survived the final liquidation of the Vileyka Jews in March of 1942.

One night I awoke to the sound of church bells ringing loudly in my ears. It was as if the bells of all the churches in town were tolling at once. I lay where I was for a long time trying to comprehend why church bells would be ringing in the middle of the night. Soon my head ached and my temples throbbed. This, coupled with the difficulty I had raising my head off the pillow, finally made me realize I was experiencing carbon monoxide poisoning. I was familiar with the symptoms because, when growing up, I had heard many stories of people found unconscious or even dead as the result of a poorly ventilated stove that allowed the poisonous gas to build up. I forced myself to get on my feet and wake up the others. The girl, Henia, and the old woman were only half conscious, but they revived quickly when we took them out into the fresh air outside. It was a narrow escape for all of us.

The month of March 1942 arrived. It wasn't spring yet. There was still plenty of snow on the ground and the nights were still cold. But the relentless grip of the winter cold had eased and the days were getting slightly, but noticably, warmer. A definite promise of spring was in the air. The festival of Purim was only a few days away.

News began filtering in that Jews were being massacred in several towns. Some massacres were partial and lasted only a day or two. Whoever got caught during the roundup was eliminated, but those who survived by escaping or hiding were allowed to return and resume their lives in town. After such an "action" (*aktion*, the Germans called it), the authorities usually put the few surviving Jews into a ghetto. Some towns went through several such purges before the Germans pronounced them *Judenrein*, that is, "clear of Jews." The final massacre ran for as long as necessary. With many non-Jewish neighbors assisting, Jews were discovered hiding in attics, under floorboards, behind double walls, and in many other ingenious places. Some Jews managed to avoid discovery for days, even weeks. But in the end, unless they were able to slip away without being seen and reach the safety of the woods, they were discovered. One could not stay in hiding in the middle of a town forever. And the chances of getting out of a hiding place and away were best the first night. As the searches got more thorough, the chances of getting away diminished steadily each successive night.

The Germans explained away the partial massacres with some excuse or other and assured the survivors they were now safe. It didn't necessarily follow that the Germans were believed, but what else could Jews do? Where else could they go? People always hoped that the next time they'd again manage to hide or escape. At this time the woods afforded at best only temporary safety because there were few partisans there. The measure of protection the partisans would eventually provide didn't materialize until the end of the summer of 1942. During the first half of 1942, few Jews chose to stay in the woods permanently. Survivors of partial "actions" usually returned to the towns they lived in. The few survivors of complete and final "actions" sought refuge in towns that had not yet been touched by the full German fury.

Then came the news that the Jews of the town of Volozin, where my oldest married sister, Sarah, had been living for ten years, had also been executed. A faint ray of hope still remained in my heart at the time; maybe by some miracle she had survived. But of course the bitter truth was that she perished in the massacre of the great majority of the Volozin Jews. After the war a survivor told me about it.

We still hoped, no matter how weakly, that somehow we would live to see the Germans defeated, a defeat we all believed would eventually occur. Slowly but surely, however, the ultimate German plan for the Jews was becoming clear to us. They intended to empty all captured lands of all Jews. It took time for this realization to crystallize, but it was a conclusion everybody came to sooner or later—except those who consciously chose to close their eyes and ears to logic and reality. Unfortunately, there were many people in this category. Their way of coping with the situation was to say that Jews should carefully avoid provoking the Germans and conscientiously perform the tasks the Germans assigned to them. Then the Germans would leave them alone. These people refused to believe the word reaching us about all the massacres or, rather, they found ways to explain away what was happening—as if there could be a rational explanation for the murder of a whole town of Jews. But this was the road to survival these distressed people chose.

I remember one case clearly. This particular Jew was about forty years old and came from a town about fifty kilometers away. The Germans had just murdered all the Jews they could get their hands on there, including the man's wife and children. He was lucky enough to escape with his life and somehow or other made it to Vileyka. I happened to meet him one day while he was telling his story and giving his opinion that the Germans would eventually do the same to every Jew in every town.

I saw no reason to disbelieve the man, and I did not entirely disagree with his assessment of what was awaiting us. Yes, it did sound extreme, but it also sounded plausible. Some of the younger people who were there and heard the man speak felt more or less the same way I did. Others, however, said the man was crazy and suggested that the terrible loss of his family had made him deranged. Young single people still had a sense of freedom of action and tended to see things differently than men who were weighed down with the responsibilities of caring for a wife and children and felt there was no way they could run off to the woods, where the hardships of existence would be multiplied many times over. They put all their hopes into doing good work for the Germans and in making themselves as useful as possible. They actually tried to block out any information that might contradict their false assessment of the situation. Then came the festival of Purim.

We couldn't celebrate Purim in any really traditional way, of course. In the evening I read the *Megilla* (Book of Esther), which is read in all synagogues in normal times. The best we could do was to gather together a few of the neighbors, who made the trip to our house through backyards. They were mostly women and a couple of young girls. After the reading we all exchanged wishes that the latter-day Haman should meet the fate of the original one. Then everybody went back home and we bedded down for the night. Except for its being Purim, this was an evening like any other.

Later we recognized the pattern, but by the time we did, most of the Jews had already perished. The pattern was that most German "actions" against Jews were carried out on Jewish holy days or, in order to confuse us, a few days before or after a holy day. Soviet Russian holidays could also trigger these "actions."

Thus, around three in the morning of Purim, 1942, I was suddenly awakened by a loud banging on the front door. This door was never used in the winter and the snow on the steps normally lay fresh and untrampled. So I knew from the first what the knocking meant. "This is it," I remember thinking. "The SD have come for us."

The animal instinct for self-preservation takes over automatically in time of danger. My first thought was to run. "Maybe out the back door," I thought. I started to put on my pants in the dark. I always used to leave my clothes on a stool next to where I slept so they would be handy in case of an emergency. I grabbed what I thought were my pants, which I usually left on top, and tried to get into them. In the excitement and terror of the moment, I couldn't get my foot through the leg. Then there was knocking at the back door. Somebody opened it and Germans came in. The kerosene lamp was lit and there I was standing half-naked with my shirt in my hands. No wonder I hadn't been able to get my foot into the sleeve.

The Germans told us to finish dressing. We were facing three huge men in SD uniforms, with the dreaded skull on their caps. All carried submachine guns. They led us out the back door and into the yard. There we were confronted by three more SD men, making six of them all told. There were seven of us—the two women and the five of us painters. The SD men marched us out of the yard and into the street towards a truck visible about a block away. A full moon glowed in the sky and the light it gave was intensified by reflections off the snow that lay on the ground. It was bright enough to read a newspaper. "Once we get to that truck we're doomed," I remember thinking. "I must keep my eyes open for a good time and spot, and then I'll make a run for it."

At one point I was all set to make the fateful sprint, and had even taken the first step, but something held me back. I suddenly realized there was no way I could have gotten away. And lucky for me I didn't try. I would have been cut down before taking a few steps.

We got to the truck and were ordered to climb in. A few people were there already and more were arriving all the time. In only five minutes the truck was filled to capacity. Canvas flaps at the back and on the sides were lowered. We stood in total darkness with guards on the truck all around us. Then the truck started moving. We couldn't tell what direction it was going in, but it did not really matter. There was no question in our minds that we were being taken to our deaths. We were more seasoned now; eight months under the Germans had dispelled much of our earlier naiveté. Now we knew just what we could expect. We said goodbye to each other. I stopped thinking about trying to flee because I knew by this time it would be impossible.

About ten minutes later the truck stopped. The canvas flaps were raised and we were ordered out. The place was well lit with artificial light. As we got off the truck, one by one, we were yelled at to run a gauntlet of SD men holding wooden clubs about the size of baseball bats. Two rows of facing SD men stretched from the truck to a building about thirty meters away. The building turned out to be a large garage, and I now recognized we were inside the SD compound that included the jail, the courthouse, and this garage. This was the dreaded place with the one-way ticket reputation.

To keep us moving, the SD men swung the clubs at and around our heads and shoulders. I made it through without getting hit. Others weren't so lucky. Several had received wounds that were bleeding profusely. Others, who had taken blows to the head, were in a semi-stunned condition. There was a purpose in all that yelling and swinging of clubs and making us run the gauntlet. It was not primarily to inflict pain or injury but to confuse us psychologically so that we could not orient ourselves or take stock of the situation. In this way no one would think of bolting. Cow-boys use the same tactic herding cattle. All the noise and shooting in the air are for the purpose of driving the startled animals in the desired direction.

Once inside the garage, we were put in a corner and told to wait. Diagonally across from us, in the opposite corner of the garage, I saw a large group of about 300 people, mostly women and children. The "action" was in full swing now. Trucks arrived bringing more and more people, who were then driven into the garage. This continued all through the night and most of the following day.

We heard later that some people had not been picked up by the SD that first night. Jewish houses were obviously on a list prepared well in advance. But by faulty intelligence or simple oversight some houses had been missed. The good luck of these Jews was short-lived, however. The next morning they started to walk to work, unaware of what had taken place during the night. They were then picked up on their way to work, or where they worked if they got that far, and trucked off to the garage.

Many of the Jews rounded up were originally from Kurenits, and a large number were young women working at menial jobs in Vileyka. One way or another they were all swept up by the "action." In the garage, smaller groups of Jews stood around and apart from the large group. I recognized the chief of the SD as he walked up to one of these smaller groups. He talked to the people there and one by one motioned with his hand for them to join the large group. Within a few minutes he had disposed of all the small groups in this way—by making them a part of the large group—all except ours. We were still standing apart. The chief of the SD now approached us. My knees felt weak. With a flick of his finger this man had sent who knows how many people to their deaths with no more emotion than it takes to swat a fly. Over 300 people in just the last hour or two. And in his whole career, maybe as many as 100,000! Yet to hear the man talk you would think him the gentlest and most civilized person in the world who could not possibly wish you any harm.

"*Wo arbeiten Sie?* (What is your place of work?),'' he politely asked the first person he reached in our group, using the formal and polite *Sie* instead of the informal and intimidating *du*. To address somebody as *Sie* in German indicates a modicum of deference, especially when coupled with the honeyed tones the chief now used.

"*Wo arbeiten Sie?*'' each person in our group was asked in turn and all answered. The older ones who didn't work said so. The chief's finger flicked in the direction of the large group. People who had work said where it was: the post office, the German police station, other offices. In all, about ten different places of work were mentioned. The chief's response was the same to all—a flick of his finger towards the main group.

When the chief finally got to one of us painters, the answer to his question was, "I'm a painter and I work for the *Gebietskommisar* (provincial governor).'' This time the finger didn't move. "Have you the certificate to prove it?'' the chief asked. We each took out the certificates that stated we were working for the *Gebietskommissar* as painters, each certificate bearing the signature of a high-ranking official and the stamp of the *Gebietskommisar*. They had been given to us just two weeks earlier. The SD chief glanced at the certificates and told the five of us to stand apart by ourselves.

A tiny glimmer of hope kindled within us. We hadn't been put in with the main group that was obviously marked for death. I nourished that small flame of hope. Maybe, just maybe, he would let us live. It was far from a sure thing, of course; we were still in the hands of the SD, in the center of the infamous SD facility from which, so far as we knew, no Jew had ever come out alive. And what was to prevent the chief from changing his mind? Or to prevent one of his men from throwing us in with the others by oversight or malice?

Presently we were led into a small side room; there we joined eleven other people who had been picked out of previous truckloads. Later, we were joined by one more couple. Besides the five of us, two others, carpenters, were from Kurenits. The rest were from Vileyka: two saddlers with their wives and one twelve-year-old son, one candle-maker and his wife, one soapmaker and his wife, and, I believe, one printer and his wife. All told there were eighteen of us in the room.

We began to hear shooting outside and saw a yellow-reddish light coming through the small barred window high up near the ceiling, as it usually is in jails. We wanted to get up to the window to see what was happening outside. There was nothing in the room to stand on, so I hopped onto somebody's shoulders. We realized this was danger-ous. If caught, we would probably have to join those outside. But the desire to know, if we could, what was going on was strong. I watched for no more than a minute.

What I saw were two SD men, each one leading a group of three people towards the fire. One group was close to the fire. The other group was just leaving the building. The fire came from the infamous pit about which we already knew.

And then I jumped down, glad we hadn't been caught watching. We heard shooting again and knew what it meant. The shooting continued throughout the rest of the night and through most of the next day.

Once, around midday, the door to our little room swung open and two Lithuanian SD burst in. They were drunk and their glassy eyes looked full of murder. In their foreign-sounding German one of them said, "*Was machen die Scheisse hier?* (What are you shit doing here?)" For a moment or two we thought we'd had it. Luckily a superior officer happened by and ordered the men out of there and to leave us alone.

The day dragged on. No food or water was brought to us, but worry and tension depressed our appetites anyway and nobody felt hungry. Early in the evening the door finally opened and an officer came in. He announced that we were going to be released and told us to step back into the main garage.

How different the place looked now from when we had been brought in. The whole main group of Jews was gone. They had all been shot and burned not more than 150 meters from where we had spent the last fifteen hours. They had been taken out in small groups to the burning pit, shot with small-caliber weapons, and then shoved into the flaming hole in the ground. All of those brought in after us, even during the day, met the same fate. I'm not certain of the exact number of those that perished in this "action," but judging by the size of the Jewish population of Vileyka before the war, it could have been as many as 2,000, including the fifty Jews from Kurenits who were also killed. Eighteen people out of 2,000 were spared by the SD; eleven of the eighteen were natives of Vileyka.

But the garage was not entirely empty. Two women, both strikingly good-looking, were now where the main group had once stood. One was from Kurenits, Khayke Rabunski, who had gone to school with me and who, as I have recounted earlier, was looking out of the window as I was led by, coming from the Lubanye farm on Simchas Torah in October 1941. The other woman was a native of Vileyka, intelligent and cultured, and perhaps in her late twenties, with a teaching degree. To what purpose these two had been kept back, we could only speculate.

When we were marched back out into the big garage, the two women stood there facing us about seven or eight meters away. Khayke called out my name a couple of times in a hoarse whisper and asked me to let people know at the police station, where she worked, what had happened, in the hope they would come to her rescue. She repeated this plea several times, not being sure whether or not we had heard it. Poor soul, we couldn't even acknowledge with a nod that we had. We were afraid of antagonizing the Germans and imperiling our own chances for release. But the possibility that someone at the police station would come to Khayke's rescue was nonexistent. The power of the SD was so great and their latitude of activity so broad that even high-ranking German officials were afraid to take them on. SD authority went unquestioned.

In the almost empty garage, a German officer sat behind a long table covered from end to end with all sorts of valuables—gold, diamonds and other jewels, stacked in places a foot high and made up of rings, bracelets, brooches, pins, chains, earrings, and watches, perhaps weighing a good twenty-five kilos. Obviously it had all been taken from the victims before they were killed. The German officer asked us if any of our valuables had been taken away and if so, we were to look through the pile and retrieve them. But none had been taken because we didn't have any. I remember thinking at the time that if anything had been taken, I certainly would not call attention to myself by asking for it. Let them keep it. We just wanted to be released.

So I was astounded to hear one man, the candlemaker, I believe, answer, "Yes." A golden pocketwatch had been taken from him and he could see it there in the pile. I was even more astounded to hear the officer tell him to go ahead and take it. The man did so.

Then the officer took our names and addresses in order to provide an escort for us back to where we lived. When he asked Irma for his address, instead of giving the street and number of the house we stayed in, Irma blurted out that we were from Kurenits. The officer responded by saying he couldn't send us back to Kurenits at night. He put the five of us painters back in the little side room to spend another night and promised to see what could be done the next day.

Back in the room, behind the locked door, we once more felt dejected and forlorn. We had been so close to freedom only to be denied it at the last minute by an unfortunate remark from one of our own. It was really more than we could bear. Who could predict how the SD would feel the next morning? Understandably, Irma felt terrible. After somebody tried to reproach him for saying what he did, he picked up a brick lying on the floor and began to hit himself on the head with it to punish himself, as if that could help us in any way. The man was really on the verge of suicide. We had our hands full just trying to quiet him down and console him.

That night was the longest I can remember. Sleep was out of the question. Again we had no food or drink and again we felt neither hunger nor thirst. We heard sporadic shooting, but on a much smaller scale.

Morning came, but there was still no sign of our being released. Several hours went by. Fresh doubts arose about the outcome of this drama; if they intended to release us, then why were they still holding us? That was the nagging question at the back of our minds and it had no satisfactory explanation.

Then about eleven in the morning the door finally opened. An officer called us out into the garage. This time it was really empty. The long table was still there but now it lay bare. The valuables that 2,000 people had accumulated over several generations had now been transferred into the coffers of the German Reich. Of course the real tragedy was the 2,000 Jews consigned to oblivion, their lives extinguished by the flick of one man's finger to satisfy the bloodlust of the leader of the *Herrnvolk* (master race) and his henchmen. The two women—one a schoolmate and lifelong friend—had disappeared to who knows what fate before they, too, would be killed.

A mere thirty hours before, these people had been live human beings, each with their own aspirations and, above all, a desire to survive. I had known many of them personally and some had been close friends. Gone now was the family at whose house I had slept for two months recently. Gone were the neighbors who had come to hear me chant the *Megilla*: the older women and the two young daughters of one of the women, sixteen and seventeen years old, both of them redheads, beautiful, and intelligent. Gone too were our landlady and the young woman from Kurenits who had prepared our meals. All of them gone. Despite all this and despite the ordeal we had just been through, we simply felt happy we were still alive and elated that we were being released.

At the place we were taken to on the outskirts of Vileyka the Germans created a ghetto. Sixty families had been brought in from Kurenits, all headed by artisans, or, as they were called at the time, *Spezialisten* (skilled workers): tailors, shoemakers, carpenters, blacksmiths, sheet-metal workers, glaziers, and others the Germans had need for. All were allowed to bring along their wives and their children up to the age of fifteen.

The ghetto consisted of two long buildings the Russians had originally built as army barracks. The buildings were in a sorry state, without doors or windows, but we were moved in anyway. We were given permission to take what we needed from Jewish houses in Vileyka, now all unoccupied since the Purim "action." Within a few days, doors and windows were found and fitted and the barracks were made more livable. Officially, we were known as the *Gebietskommissarsgetto* (provincial governor's ghetto) because we worked for the *Gebietskommissar*.

Only real, experienced mechanics were brought to Vileyka and they came eagerly, even though it meant exchanging homes with many rooms and familiar surroundings for the cramped corner of a dormitory that had to be shared with several other families and that was without privacy or conveniences. It would also have been easier to cope with the food situation in Kurenits, where people knew some non-Jews and where bartering of clothing and articles for food would have been easier than in Vileyka, where all the people and surroundings were unfamiliar. Officially, Jews were prohibited from any social or business contacts with non-Jews; in Kurenits this would have been easier to circumvent because many Jewish houses were located in among the others.

Nonetheless, all these workers and their families were quite happy to move to Vileyka. By this time it was understood that working for the *Gebietskommissar* in Vileyka afforded some measure of protection. Not absolute protection—few were naive enough to believe that—but a measure of protection for the immediate future. News of the Vileyka Purim massacre, together with rumors and reports of Jews being wiped out in other neighboring towns, made Kurenits's Jews realize that Kurenits afforded no protection at all, even for workers. Sooner or later Kurenits would follow the same fate as the other towns.

Our two master painters, Yosef and Irma, brought their wives and children to Vileyka to be with them. About twelve of us, mostly young and unmarried, shared one room, sleeping on army cots. After some breakfast in the morning, we all—except the married women and the children—went to work and did not return until dark.

After a few days I managed to take off from work and go visit my family in Kurenits. This time, however, unlike all previous times, I had no official permission to go to Kurenits, much less to be absent from the new ghetto.

The route to Kurenits from the ghetto required crossing the entire town of Vileyka from one end to the other, a distance of about one and a half kilometers. There was, however, little danger in walking the streets of Vileyka because both the police and the Germans were used to seeing Jewish workers walking from one job to another. Once outside of town, though, you had to negotiate seven kilometers of public highway between the two towns. Here the danger was greater but still acceptable. Vehicles with Germans passed by and you could never be too sure whether they might take into their heads to "stop that wandering Jew." To forestall identification by taking off the yellow star of David we displayed on our clothes, front and back, could have proved even more dangerous. I actually worried more about meeting up with the non-German policemen who sometimes traveled the road to Kurenits on bicycles. I kept a sharp lookout for them and whenever I spotted any in the distance, I hid in the bushes by the side of the road until they had passed.

In this way I arrived back home safely and was enthusiastically greeted by my parents and sisters. They had learned, as had everybody else in Kurenits, about the events in Vileyka on Purim from one Kurenits carpenter working in Vileyka just like us. He happened to wake up in the middle of the night of the "action" and, hearing all the commotion in the street, he got out as fast as he could. Using backyards and side streets he crossed the town of Vileyka and reached Kurenits before dawn, unchallenged. Within an hour the whole town of Kurenits buzzed with the news. At first, for a period of thirty-six to forty-eight hours, my family assumed I was among the dead. Then they heard I had been released. Naturally they were quite relieved to receive the news and anxious to see me. I stayed overnight in Kurenits and returned to Vileyka the next day.

Back in Vileyka I found the people in a somewhat more optimistic frame of mind. The living quarters in the ghetto barracks had been made more livable with the addition of a table and a couple of extra chairs. There were even curtains at the windows of our room, courtesy of the young women. This better mood came mostly as a result of feeling that we had just been handed a new lease on life—not permanent, or even long-term, but what we hoped would last for a while at least. The Germans wouldn't go to all the trouble of bringing in master craftsmen and allowing us to fix up the ghetto buildings unless they needed us. So went the thinking and there was some logic in it.

Spring had just begun and the weather was getting warmer. The often sunny days that followed also played a part in helping to lift our spirits. With the full encouragement of the Germans we built a small bathhouse between the two barracks. Germans were sticklers for cleanliness. They were afraid of epidemics that uncleanliness might bring on.

For me the euphoric feeling didn't last very long. One day, when I came home from work and walked into our room, I noticed that all conversation among the ten people present came to an abrupt halt. I didn't pay much attention to it at first, though it did seem odd. The next day I also noticed some whispering going on among the people around me. When I tried to join a group that was engrossed in conversation, they quickly separated. My questions were answered in a vague and offhand manner. I got the feeling that information was deliberately being kept from me and it all pointed in the direction of my family in Kurenits. Something must have happened, perhaps something terrible.

I decided then and there to leave for Kurenits in the morning and find out for myself what was up. It had been three weeks since my last visit back home and it was no longer possible to move between Vileyka and Kurenits as easily as before. Ghetto residents had been forbidden to be absent from the ghetto for any reason at all except work.

So the next morning I left the place I was working, with the other painters covering for me. Getting across Vileyka still presented no problem. Once outside of town I turned to the right off the main road, went through some fields, and reached a small village (the name of which I have since forgotten). There I picked up a small farm road leading almost the rest of the way to Kurenits. This detour added about two or three extra kilometers but was safer since I met no one at all the whole way.

My apprehension grew with each step as I approached my hometown. I could sense that something disastrous must have happened there, but I could not imagine the extent of it. As I entered the town square, I noticed Jews in the distance walking and going about their business in a quite normal manner. This confused me, but gave me a slight measure of hope that maybe this had all been a false alarm after all.

I soon ran into my friend Nyomke Shulman and asked, "Tell me what's happened. Has anyone been killed?"

"Well," he answered evasively, "there are no exact figures yet. Many people ran away. And some of them haven't come back. It's not known how many are missing."

"What about my family? Are they all right?"

"Yes," he said. "Your mother is at the house of Zalman Mendl the shoemaker."

I didn't have to inquire any further. Without telling me outright, Nyomke had indirectly indicated the extent of the disaster.

I ran all the way to Zalman Mendl's house. There I found my mother holding little Shimshon, Minya's son, on her lap. Mother's eyes were puffy and red. She burst out crying again when she saw me and we cried in each other's arms for a long time. Shimshon, even when he was not crying, looked hopelessly sad and forlorn. This was not the happy baby who used to greet me with a big smile. His face showed how much he missed his mother. It was as if he understood. And now I too knew what the tragedy was. All that was left was for Mother to tell me how it had happened.

The disaster had struck two days earlier, at about ten in the morning. Without warning, two Polish policemen, both of them drunk, barged into the house. They ordered everybody, except Mother, out into the backyard—my father, my sister Ethel, and my sister Minn with the baby in her arms. Then they shot Father and Minn dead. The baby fell from Minn's lifeless arms into the snow. Ethel tried to run away. She made it through an opening in the fence and across the street into another yard. There one of the policemen caught up with her and shot her dead, too. Mother was standing by the kitchen window and saw everything. There had to be an added measure of deliberate cruelty in murdering a woman's husband and children before her very eyes.

These policemen were not only accustomed to cruelty, they positively reveled in it. One, Blizniuk, was a native of Kurenits; he was the same policeman who had hauled me out of the Lubanye farm in the fall of 1941 and who, the same day, had shot Arke Ruvkes as he lay wounded on the ground. The man had got a taste of blood then and apparently he liked it. The other policeman, from Kostenevich, a small town about seventeen kilometers away, was named Szarenkiewicz. He had participated in the killing of the fifty-four on Simchas Torah of 1941 and had also taken part in the liquidation of the Vileyka Jews on Purim. Besides my sisters and father, the pair of them had murdered twenty-nine other Jews in Kurenits, a total of thirty-two.

After the two policemen left, Mother went outside and lifted the terrified baby up out of the snow. She was helped to move into Zalman Mendl's so she would not have to live by herself with the baby in the house where the murders had occurred. Father and Minn were buried the next day in the Jewish cemetery outside of town. By the time I got to Kurenits only Ethel remained unburied, and with the help of a couple of men, we laid her to rest next to my father and Minya.

Artsik Gotyes, a friend of the family, was one of those who helped in the burial of all three members of my family. He handed me a piece of paper he had taken from my father's pocket. On the paper were listed all the names, and other detailed information, of the fifty-four victims who perished in the fall of 1941. To this list we now added the names of the thirty-two who had just been killed. I kept the paper on me for a long time, until it finally disintegrated over the next couple of years.

Yitskhok (Iche Hatsyes), my father, was about sixty-three years old when he was murdered. He was highly respected by both the Jewish community and the gentiles. He was a recognized scholar in all the holy scriptures, including the Talmud. He knew Hebrew and Russian and had a good knowledge of mathematics. He was a teacher most of his life and even taught Russian and mathematics in our public school and in night school. The policeman who shot him, Blizniuk, had once been a student of his in night school. To me he was more than a father; he was also my teacher, from the age of five through the age of fourteen, in all nonsecular subjects. He had a unique talent in explaining difficult passages in the scriptures in such a way as to make them easy to understand. His lectures on *Mishna* and *Gemara* were very much appreciated and well attended. He was considered a special authority on these subjects and he was even consulted on some difficult and tricky passages of law by the local rabbi. He had a sharp, analytical mind and all who knew him acknowledged him to be a brilliant scholar.

As a young teenager I never ceased to be amazed at my father's ability to demolish every argument an opponent in a discussion could come up with. He answered with such ease and logic that everyone present was soon won over, including the opponent. He also possessed a beautiful voice and was a cantor. His rendition and interpretation of the prayers, especially on the High Holidays, were deeply moving and soul-inspiring. He was also an excellent *bal kriah*—reader of the Torah. People who had the privilege of hearing him read the Torah and chant while leading the congregation in prayer still speak of it with a praise reserved for masters of these crafts.

It is told that an important Talmudic discussion once took place in Kurenits between a visiting rabbi from the city of Lublin and our local rabbi and several local scholars, my father among them. The topic was one aspect of a certain work by *Rambam* Maimonides. It was not unusual for this kind of discussion to last for several hours, as the learned men brought out and carefully analyzed all the fine points of law and brought to bear the many commentaries, all in the presence of a large congregation that would gather for such an event. At the end of this discussion the visiting rabbi turned to the congregation and, pointing to my father, said: "Here in Kurenits you have a priceless pearl. You should consider yourselves blessed by his presence among you." This took place when I was still a little boy and too young to know of it at firsthand, but it is related in a chapter by Abraham Dimentstein (Avrohom Merkes) in the book *Megilat Kurenits* (edited by Aaron Meirovitch 1956).

And now my father was gone. No longer would I be able to listen to his wise counsel or, with the numerous other students of his, children as well as adults, be able to drink at the deep well of knowledge he possessed.

Gone, too, were my two sisters Ethel and Minn, at the ages of thrity-one and twenty-eight. Ethel was a pretty brunette, the brainiest one among my sisters. Minya, my favorite, was not only very pretty but also gentle, warm, very loyal to the family, and well-liked and well-thought of by all who came in contact with her. My sisters were cut down by two drunken policemen, eager for Jewish blood.

If there is any consolation, it is in the knowledge that some measure of justice came down on the pair of killers. They soon received their just due. One, the native of Kurenits, was killed four months later by partisans. The other was dispatched by the SD, for whom he often worked so diligently, into the same flaming pit into which he himself had helped send so many of the Jews of Vileyka. One day, during the summer of 1942, thinking that killing was easy and looked upon with favor by the Germans, he took it upon himself to settle a few private accounts of his own with some of his fellow townsfolk he had quarreled with at one time or another. He went out and shot a dozen and a half of them, all non-Jews, since no Jews were left in Kostenevich. He apparently saw little difference between killing Jews and non-Jews. The Germans, however, did make the distinction. They picked him up immediately, put a bullet in his neck, and tossed him into the pit.

Now there was only Mother and the baby and I left in our family. I stayed overnight in Kurenits and went away the next day. Much as I hated to leave Mother and the baby, I simply had to show up for work or I would be in trouble with the Germans. Mother was so anxious for me to get back to Vileyka that she urged me to leave at once without even staying the night. She knew Vileyka was safer than Kurenits. Taking the same backroads route, I returned to the Vileyka ghetto without incident.

4

The population of the Vileyka ghetto kept expanding while the available living space remained the same. When the ghetto was first formed, it consisted mainly of Kurenits people. They were soon joined by skilled artisans and their families from other towns who arrived in increasing numbers. Everybody had to be accommodated in the same two buildings, so the amount of living space per person shrank constantly, resulting in serious overcrowding.

Many other new workers from various trades joined our ghetto. A few had been ordered in just for their skills from Jewish communities that were still intact; most were remnants of recently destroyed communities. In some of the "actions," the Germans would leave a few craftsmen alive, depending on what expertise was needed at that particular moment. These men, who had been spared for their skill and experience, were then brought to Vileyka. Some, however, were not really craftsmen but simply passed themselves off as such.

By the time the summer of 1942 arrived, the population of the ghetto had swelled from the original sixty families to almost double that number—110 families, or about 240 people. This was an open ghetto in that it had no fences around it and, most important, no guards. Theoretically, you could pretty much come and go at will. In practice, though, it wasn't at all like that. If you were stopped in the street, you had to be able to explain your absence from the ghetto. Consequently, only the workers were able to move around certain streets with relative ease.

The women were sometimes able to get food from passing farmers in exchange for a few articles of clothing or a piece of jewelry. The Germans supplied us with minimum rations—a barely adequate amount of bread and a small portion of meat per person once a week. Each family supplemented these official rations as best they could. So the food situation, while far from good, was tolerable.

In the middle of the summer about twenty of us young men from different Zionist groups organized a night watch. We stood guard on a three-hour rotation and were prepared to sound the alarm in case the Germans were seen approaching. I had misgivings about it from the start but went along anyway. I didn't question the reasons for setting it up—these were valid enough—as much as I questioned its effectiveness. The ghetto was situated in such a way that you could not see more than half a city block away in any one direction even during the day, let alone at night. If Germans actually did come for us, we wouldn't see them until it would be too late to figure out their true intent or do anything effective about it. After a month the guard was discontinued as others also came to realize that the effort was futile.

I was able to get back to Kurenits to visit my mother and my little nephew about once every three or four weeks. From visit to visit I saw the overall situation deteriorate. Superficially, everything appeared the same. Kurenits was still a free town and no ghetto had been set up in it. As a rule the police did not harass the Jews and no Germans were stationed in town. Everything seemed calm—too calm, the calm before the storm. Jews felt in their bones what was coming as surely as some animals sense an earthquake is impending. Most of the towns around Kurenits had already suffered one or more "actions" or, worse, total destruction. People's nerves were frayed. The smallest rumor or misunderstood remark was enough to trigger a panic.

A number of false alarms in Kurenits sent people scurrying out into the woods. It usually started when somebody thought they overheard some official say that the Germans might be coming. That was all it took to set off the chain reaction. Most of these rumors were out-and-out false, others only partially so.

I was caught up in one of these false alarms around December 1941, when my father and sisters were still alive. I remember it was cold and there was snow on the ground. On one of my regular weekend visits from Vileyka I suddenly saw two men running and yelling that the Germans were coming and that they were going to surround the town. I ran back into my house, gave the warning, and then ran out into the fields, heading towards the village of Pukyen and the woods beyond. I was joined by two more young men and together we made it to the woods about two kilometers away, on the other side of Pukyen. There we spent the whole day wondering what was happening back in Kurenits. We heard no shooting and we could observe nothing out of the ordinary. By evening we decided to return and approached the town cautiously and soon found out the whole thing had been just another false alarm. There were more of them as time went by.

Another, more serious "false alarm" that proved not to be so false occurred in January 1942. Some important-looking German officials arrived in Kurenits from Vileyka and ordered the police to round up about fifty Jews and bring them to the town square. Word spread fast and many young people got to the woods. (I was in Vileyka when it happened and heard the story later.) The police rounded up the required number of people, mostly older men, my father among them. When they got to the town square, they were made to disrobe from the waist up and the Jewish community was ordered to hand over a certain quantity of furs. The hostages were kept standing half-naked in near-zero-degree weather for three hours until enough furs were turned over to the Germans. No one was killed or taken away.

Even after so many rehearsals, most people were genuinely taken by suprise when the real performance came. If anything, the false alarms had dulled the senses, as with the proverbial "boy who cried wolf."

The survival rate among the Jews of Kurenits, relative to that of surrounding towns, was greater because their destruction came comparatively late, three days before Rosh Hashana in 1942, giving people more time to prepare for the inevitable and to devise or construct hiding places, some of them quite ingenious. We called such a place a *malina* (hiding place) or a *skhron* (shelter). It would usually be stocked with enough food and water to last the people inside for a couple of days. The most popular kind of hiding place was constructed under the floor of one of the rooms of a house. By pulling up two or three of the twenty-five-centimeter floorboards, you gained access to a large hole that had been dug underneath and that was sometimes able to accommodate as many as ten to twelve people. Some shelters were built by pooling the energies and efforts of two or more households. All the sand and other debris created when the hole was dug had to be hauled away by hand, in small quantities, so as not to raise suspicions. The debris was then deposited and camouflaged to make it as unnoticable as possible.

Another way of creating a good hiding place was to erect a false wall several feet out from an existing one, in the cellar, or the attic, or wherever else the layout of a building lent itself to. Again, building materials such as wood or bricks and cement had to be obtained and brought in surreptitiously and the debris disposed of in the same manner. Special attention had to be given to ventilation and lighting.

People constructed other kinds of shelters, too. They dug holes in their backyards and camouflaged them as best they could. Of course, to be able to use the hiding place once it was constructed, you had to have the extra bit of good luck of finding out that danger was at hand in time to enter the hole and close it up before being detected.

Some people hired one of the local Jewish masons to build more elaborate hiding places for them. This approach had its own problems and dangers. Secrecy was obviously of the utmost importance and the more people, including a mason, who were aware of a particular hiding place, the less secure it became, no matter what other qualities it might possess. In the town of Dolhinov a mason had been coerced into revealing all the hiding places he had built for people.

It is safe to say that a large segment of the Jewish population of Kurenits prepared themselves a hiding place of one kind or another. Of course, not every shelter was constructed perfectly; even the best laid plans sometimes go awry. A lot depended on luck. A house might have the best possible hiding place, but if the house was among the first that the Germans selected to surround and enter, then the inhabitants might very well not have time enough to go through all the steps necessary to disappear inside it. Moreover, if such a hiding place was also meant to serve several households, its usefulness to the others evaporated at the same time.

Some people were discovered because of inadequate camouflaging or because of an inadvertent noise, such as a man coughing or a child crying. Other people were given away by the noise they made when they tried to come out. Other people were discovered by locals engaged in the sport of ferreting out Jews and, not incidentally, getting their hands on Jewish possessions. Finally, still other people failed in their attempts to hide out during an "action" through a combination of circumstances that can only be called plain bad luck.

I continued to visit my mother and my nephew as often as I could, even though it was risky to travel between Vileyka and Kurenits, or even just to be in Kurenits. I no longer stayed overnight. At this stage people realized that "actions" typically began during the night or just before dawn, when most people were still asleep.

Each time I came to Kurenits, Mother used to ask me to go and visit our old house with her. It was a large house, quite possibly the largest in town, and had been built in 1926 after the great fire of the previous year reduced most of the town to ashes. Its massive concrete walls were about two feet thick and it contained twelve rooms. After we went into the house, Mother would go from room to room, weeping bitterly. She examined every corner of every room almost as if she expected to find her lost husband and children again.

I made my last visit to Kurenits just two weeks before the "action" that destroyed the Kurenits Jews, my mother and little Shimshon among them. Judl, my fellow painter, and I went together and this final visit ended differently from all the others.

The rest of the painters opposed our going and informed the ghetto leader, Schatz, about what we had done. Schatz was on friendly terms with one particular German officer, who when told of the problem, drove with Schatz to Kurenits to round us up. They located us easily. Before driving us back, the German gave us a tongue-lashing on the spot and a slap across the face, which apparently closed the incident for him. But for my mother, this was the last she ever saw of me—her son being publicly demeaned and carried off by a German.

The Germans decided to have a tennis court built. The order for this particular project, came from one Herr Hendl, the deputy *Gebietskommissar*. Twenty of us worked on this tennis court project Saturdays and Sundays for several weeks. First we had to break up several truckloads of bricks into fragments no larger than a half-inch in size. This was hard, tedious work with the inadequate tools we had at our disposal—plain rocks and a couple of hammers. Then all that red rubble had to be spread out evenly and rolled smoothly into the ground with a large steel roller. It took four or five of us at a time to push and pull the thing back and forth across the area. But we ended up with a nice red tennis court that had the required smooth, hard surface. It was pleasing to the eye and met the needs of the game. Herr Hendl and his friends seemed to be quite satisfied with it.

Once the Germans started playing, however, they soon realized the court did have one flaw. It was surrounded by an old fence that was not quite high enough for a proper game of tennis. The balls kept going over the fence and into the street on one end of the court or into the landscape at the other. The delays caused in retrieving the tennis balls proved annoying to the officers and risked spoiling the sport for them. But the Germans rose to the occasion and solved this inconvenience with exemplary Nazi ingenuity. A number of young and agile Jews were sent for and required to be present when the court was in use. They were stationed around the outside of the court but inside the fence. When a ball went over the fence, so did one of us to fetch it and throw it back in to the players. The distance and direction of our throw had better be right. When judged a poor throw by one of the officers, the offending thrower received "physical encouragement" to strive towards German excellence.

One day in June 1942 the Germans started feverish preparations to spruce up the Vileyka theater for some upcoming production or other. A Polish engineer, who was also a stage expert, was brought in from Molodechno to design the scenery and install a new curtain. We painters spent a full week doing the interior walls. When the painting job was done, we were assigned the task of painting a great German eagle just above the proscenium arch. I got the job because I was known to have some aptitude for meticulous drawing.

I located designs for several German eagles, all of them clutching the Nazi swastika in their talons. There had been no particular instructions about which, if any, pose of the eagle was to be preferred. I assumed any would do, and selected the one that looked easiest to copy.

It took a whole day to enlarge the thing to a proper size and then to paint it on the wall. When I finally stepped back to admire my handiwork, I thought I'd done a pretty fine job and so did my fellow painters.

Next day, however, when the Germans came round to inspect the bird, they immediately burst out laughing. "*Nein, nein, Dummkopf!*" they gasped between spasms of mirth. "That's a commercial eagle, an eagle for an advertisement. What we want is the official Nazi emblem, the Nazi party eagle." They were having a fine old time laughing at my ignorance in not knowing enough to tell the two apart. The other painters then repainted the entire proscenium wall and they found they had to do it twice in order to cover my eagle enough not to show through. Two days later the correct Nazi party eagle had taken the place of the commercial bird. I was able to give it just the right expression of fierceness to satisfy my masters.

In the summer of 1942, I noticed that an elderly German officer with the help of one or two soldiers would sometimes bring boxes up to the attic of the Vileyka theater building. Once, after they left, I went upstairs and found the attic door locked. I came back with a pair of pliers and managed to pry the latch hook out of the door frame far enough for the door to open. Inside the attic I discovered many boxes of rifle rounds in their original, waterproof metal boxes. Each held over a hundred rounds. They were of Russian manufacture and had been left behind by the Russians in their hasty retreat at the beginning of the war.

On my next visit to Kurenits I talked to my friend Nokhum Alperovits about my discovery. By this time Nokhum was already a part-time member of the partisans, as were the brothers Eli and Motye Alperovits (Ruve-Zishkes), Shimon Cyrulnik, Nyomke Shulman, Ichke Einbinder, and Zalman Gurevich, and maybe one or two others. Nokhum gave me the name and address of a young Jewish woman in Vileyka who had been instrumental in recruiting them all to work with the partisans. Her name was Berta. He urged me to get in touch with her and bring her as much ammunition as possible for delivery to the partisans.

I went to see this woman and after I met her I realized how ideal she was for her work as a partisan contact. She looked like an ordinary non-Jewish farm girl and nobody in the neighborhood knew or suspected that she was Jewish. Because of this she could move around easily inside Vileyka and outside as well. She supported my plan because the partisans were then very short of ammunition.

I still had to sell my scheme to Kopel Spektor. He lived in the same room with me at the ghetto and worked as a locksmith and mechanic. He had the tools and expertise to open those metal boxes and shut them up afterwards. The plan was to open the boxes, remove the rounds, then replace them with sand of the same weight.

I proposed to bring one box of rounds back to the ghetto with me every evening. There the rounds would be taken out and replaced with sand and the next morning I would carry the box back and leave it where I had found it. This would be repeated as many times as possible. It was a dangerous scheme for me because I had to carry everything back and forth and then deliver the expropriated rounds to the other side of town.

Kopel agreed to cooperate on a trial basis. After we had taken the rounds from four boxes, about five hundred in all, everybody in our room became too jittery for us to continue and so we abandoned the scheme. I delivered this ammunition in two separate trips and conveyed our wishes that the bullets find their intended marks. Nokhum told me later that Berta did not survive the war.

One morning toward the end of July 1942, I was awakened by loud noises and screaming. Yosef, the Kurenits painter, who lived in the room across the hall from ours, burst into our room yelling that Irma, the other master painter, had just swallowed a bottle of undiluted vinegar in an apparent attempt to commit suicide. Before the war, vinegar was sold in undiluted form. You added an ounce of it to about one liter of water to make a solution of proper kitchen strength. Undiluted the acid was strong enough to burn living tissue.

Irma was lying on the floor, writhing in pain and moaning. Burn marks were visible on his lips and inside his mouth. It must have taken a lot of willpower to drink half a liter of the stuff. It was not at all the same thing as squeezing a trigger or biting down on a cyanide capsule. The pain while drinking the acid and then afterwards before losing consciousness must have been excruciating. We rushed the man to the hospital where he died about five hours later.

What made him take such a fateful and irrevocable step? Guilt, it turned out, because his wife was with child and he blamed himself. They already had two children, and obviously the times were wrong for bringing new life into the world. But the step he took did nothing to resolve any of the problems of the wife and children he left behind. By taking his own life he as good as sentenced them to death. With the artisan gone, the wife and children had no excuse to be in the Vileyka ghetto and so they were soon sent back to Kurenits, where they moved into her parents' house. Within six weeks they were dead, together with most of the Kurenits Jews. If Irma had refrained from his final act, the family's chances of survival would have been better than fifty-fifty. All the painters, except him, survived.

With the Germans' permission, we buried Irma in the Jewish cemetery in Vileyka. It took several hours to dig his grave and lay him to rest properly. The day was warm and quiet. Lulled by the peacefulness and tranquility of the cemetery, I wondered whether Irma might not in fact be better off than the rest of us. At least he had been laid to rest by good friends, in a Jewish cemetery, and with a proper Jewish burial and prayers. Who would do that for the rest of us? The Germans were liquidating Jews on an accelerated schedule. None of these victims got a decent burial; many were reduced to ashes, being burned alive. It was a time when the living envied the dead.

One day I was helping get a house ready for some German official. The walls had big holes in them where the wooden framework showed through. Our job was to undertake the difficult work of closing up those holes, replastering, and then painting all the rooms. That particular day I was working alone with Yosef Zuckerman. We talked a lot as we worked and reflected on how hopeless our situation was. "How is the world ever going to know what happened to us?" Yosef said. "By the time the Germans are defeated, no Jews will be left alive. How will the world ever know that we were systematically destroyed and how we suffered in the days before the end?"

Then he suddenly had an idea. "Let's write a long letter

describing what has already happened and how things are now and what we expect will happen to us. We'll put the letter in a bottle and slip the bottle through one of the holes in these walls and then seal it in. Nothing lasts forever," he went on. "Houses eventually fall apart and walls crack open. Someday, in fifty years or so, somebody will discover the bottle and the message inside it." So that is what we actually did. Somewhere in Vileyka, I suppose our message may still be waiting to be discovered.

Around August 1942 some of us were moved to new quarters by a sudden and unexpected order. The official reason given was overcrowding and this was true enough. The ghetto population was divided approximately in half and one part remained in the old ghetto, while the other, which included me, was moved closer to the center of town, near the offices of the *Gebietskommissar* and next door to the building that housed the workshops for the various trades. Although it was much more crowded—we slept two to a bed—we somehow felt more secure than in the old ghetto.

In September the expected thunderbolt struck. Kurenits's turn finally came. The Kurenits Jews were being destroyed. We got wind of what was happening only hours after it started. The news electrified and stunned the entire ghetto. Almost everybody had family members who were at that very moment being annihilated. People milled about aimlessly, with blank looks of despair on their faces. The women cried and moaned. The men shuffled around in shock. No work was done that day. By the time night fell, we knew it was all over.

The next day details of the Kurenits "action" began to trickle in. This had not been a partial but a "total action." It began before dawn. SD troops and the police surrounded Kurenits and began a systematic house-to-house search to flush out as many Jews as they could from homes and hiding places. Those they found were taken by force to the town square, around the perimeter of which more Germans and police stood guard. This phase of the "action" lasted until noon. Then the whole collection of Jews were herded up Myadler Street to a place outside of town where they were driven into a large barn. The barn doors were closed and a wooden bar set in place. The structure was then torched. As the conflagration grew, flaming wall boards began to fall to the ground. Those who managed to break out through these openings were shot down by the SD and police who surrounded the building. The cold ashes of victims were eventually spread over the field on which the barn had stood, and plowed under.

I went to look at this place in August 1944, after the Germans had been driven out. No sign of the barn remained, or of the 1,500 human beings who perished there, or any other remnant of the grisly deed perpetrated there. It looked like any other ordinary field of barley. When I talked to the farmer who owned the plot of land, he didn't seem unduly concerned about the recent history of his field or the part it had played in the murder of almost all the town's Jews. Quite the contrary, I had the distinct impression that the prospect of an exceptionally bountiful harvest on this well fertilized field pleased him.

Kurenits, where Jews had lived for hundreds of years, joined the ranks of many other towns in becoming *Judenrein*—cleared of Jews, a distinction eventually bestowed on every town and city in Nazi-occupied Europe.

What went on in the minds of the people in that barn from the moment someone first yelled "Fire!" to the moment the last conscious breath was drawn is not at all hard to imagine but may best be left unspoken. To dwell on it would shake the foundations of people's sanity. I refer to the sanity of the families and friends of the victims, not to the Germans, whose sanity, so far as I know, was never threatened. All the Germans, Latvians, Lithuanians, and the local Polish and White Russian police—those who actually perpetrated the murders—went unpunished. With rare exceptions they not only survived the war but went on to flourish. They continue to flourish to this day in many different countries, including the United States, countries that gave them safe haven and continue to do so despite the fact that their dark past is known and that many of them continue to live off the Jewish treasures they plundered. One of them has even been elected secretary-general of the United Nations and president of his "neutral" country.

Nor was sanity threatened among the hundreds of local non-Jews who gathered around to watch the spectacle of "their" Jews being burned alive, neighbors they had known most of their lives. When the few Jewish survivors trekked back into the town in July of 1944, after the Germans had retreated, none of the Kurenits gentiles, with rare exceptions, expressed either sorrow or regret about what had happened.

It was the day after the destruction that the realization hit home that Kurenits no longer existed and that my mother and my little nephew were no longer among the living. Almost everybody else in the ghetto had lost someone dear and close to them there. We all had to come to grips with this fact and go on with our lives as best we could.

With the exception of my youngest sister Dina, who was married and lived deep inside Russia, and of me, everyone in our family had now been wiped out. Dina, I felt, had the best chance of surviving, and before the ordeal was over might well turn out to be the sole survivor in our family. I didn't rate my own chances very high at that point.

5

Survival now took on a new meaning. It became an obsession with me and others. But the same tragedy affected different people in different ways. Some were more determined than ever to seek their salvation through more of the same old routine, that is, giving good and hard work to the Germans and being useful to them. Unbelievable as it may seem now, there were even some young people who behaved like that. Still others gave up altogether. They believed that all was lost anyway, no matter what they or anyone else might do—like a condemned man whose only remaining choice is between going to the gallows quietly and peacefully or being dragged to his fate kicking and screaming. No matter what he does, the outcome is the same.

Another group, made up mostly of young people, took the opposite view and I shared their outlook. However safe the ghetto appeared to be for the short haul, it was doomed. I saw no viable future for any Jew who remained in German hands. The only question I had about the ghetto was, "How long will it last?" Its ultimate fate was not in doubt. There was no way, I reasoned, that the Germans were going to allow us to survive when they eventually had to retreat. And the chances were greater that the ghetto would be done away with much sooner. If there was any chance at all of surviving, it would have to be outside of German control. For us that meant just one place: the forest. With this in mind I became one of the organizers of an escape from the ghetto. While our families were still alive in Kurenits, we felt constrained to put off such an undertaking lest we put their lives in jeopardy. With that last constraint removed, we started to plan our move seriously and systematically.

Several days after the Kurenits "action," we got word that some Kurenits families had successfully hidden and then had escaped and were living in a forest about eighteen kilometers outside of town. The forest was large and covered about forty square kilometers. We also got word that partisans lived in the forest. That would explain why the Germans and the police did not hunt the escaped Jews down.

More and more details about what had taken place in Kurenits during the "action," including certain episodes, began to surface. Some people had proved brave, even heroic. Others had not. Still others had simply had very bad luck. All the stories were tragic.

Zusye the shopkeeper and his wife, an older Hasidic couple, chose to commit suicide rather than allow themselves to be marched away with the others to certain death. They were childless and for many years owned and ran a notions store in the square. By town standards they were considered rich. They were obviously well prepared, because before taking the poison Zusye dressed himself in his burial garments and covered himself with his *tallis*, or prayer shawl. Their house was set on fire and their partially burned bodies were found on what was left of the bed.

Khaya-Itke Sosenski, the older daughter of Doni and Khantse Sosenski, was about sixteen. When she and a few others caught late in the "action" were brought to the barn, it was already on fire. The others, when ordered to enter the blazing structure, understandably balked. Khaya-Itke defiantly faced her executioners and spoke to them in a voice loud enough to be heard by the watching gallery of locals standing in the back, who had come to take in the show. She castigated them for murdering innocent people and told them that as surely as the sun will rise they would pay for their crime. A day of reckoning would come. After this speech, she turned around and threw herself into the flames.

Then there was the middle-aged man who was a member of the *Judenrat* and who assumed the "action" would be partial. He apparently felt secure enough not to go into hiding and was forced into revealing the *malina* where his father, mother, and sisters were hiding. The man was promised that everyone would be spared. Then he was ordered to tell them all to come out. They did so, along with five or six of the family's neighbors, and all were of course taken straightaway to the barn.

My mother and the baby and Zalman Mendl had no chance of surviving once the "action" started. They knew it and never intended to hide. Mother was fifty-eight or fifty-nine years of age at the time—not old, even by the standards of those times—but the years of long hours and hard work running our inn-and-restaurant business had taken their toll. She also had a pronounced limp, perhaps the result of polio. The tragedy of March 1942, when my father and two sisters were killed before her eyes, left her a broken woman. She could no longer walk a half a kilometer without becoming exhausted.

To escape, you had to be able to cover many kilometers on foot and, on occasion, to sprint short distances, all this just to have a fighting chance of reaching safe haven in the woods. And having got that far, you had to be physically fit enough to withstand the rigors of the long, cold Russian winter, which included sleeping on the ground on a bed of branches, surrounded by as much as a meter of snow. You also had to be psychologically fit enough to tolerate the constant fear that the Germans or the police might attack at any moment. Being young helped, of course, but it was no guarantee. Even some of the younger and apparently fit men succumbed to the hardships and died in the woods.

Zalman Mendl, the shoemaker, had been a very sick man for many years before the war. Among other things, he suffered from heart disease and advanced emphysema, and his breathing was heavy and labored. A man in this condition could never hide without drawing attention to himself. So Zalman Mendl made the decision he had to make. Then he and my mother helped hide his daughter Dishka and her husband Hershl, the son of Khona the butcher, who had chosen to go behind a heavy armoire in their bedroom. Zalman Mendl and Mother pushed it back in place after the young couple was safely ensconced behind it. The whole first day of the "action" the couple remained undiscovered. But they knew it was unlikely their hiding place would stand up very long to the searches, which would become more intense and thorough each day. That night they decided to come out and run for the woods. Then bad luck they could not have foreseen intervened.

Zalman Mendl, despite his poor state of health, was considered the best shoemaker in town, a master craftsman. Several pairs of boots and shoes, in unfinished and finished states could be found in his workshop at any time, as could various kinds of other leather goods. Most had been ordered by high-ranking officials, usually Germans. All these leather goods were very desirable but beyond the reach of the average person, so to prevent stealing or looting, the police posted a twenty-four-hour guard at the house as soon as the "action" started. When the young couple pushed the heavy armoire they were hiding behind away from the wall, the policeman on guard heard the noise they made and shot them as they emerged. In any other house but this one, their plan would have succeeded.

The parents of my friend Nyomke Sutskever, together with two or three of their neighbors, found temporary refuge in the attic of the middle synagogue in town. It was a difficult place to climb up into, but they managed somehow and stayed there for over a week, most likely without food or water. In the end they were discovered by a town gentile by the name of Valodke. He was the son of Mishke Stankiewicz, who lived among the Jews and made his living from them. The son lost no time in reporting his discovery to the police, who came and shot them. This Valodke Stankiewicz was also responsible for discovering and reporting many other Jews in hiding, who were then sent immediately to their deaths. There were many more such episodes, not all of them known to me. Some became known much later, others not until the end of the German occupation. Many stories never surfaced at all, their secrets well kept by the witnesses, the executioners, and the victims, now silent forever.

One tragic incident was related to me by Artsik Gotyes in February 1943, when I met him in a village not far from the Russian town of Ushachi and we spent the night in the hayloft of a barn. He told me how he had escaped from Kurenits and what had happened to his family. As he talked, I realized that this was more a confession than a story. His heart was obviously laden with guilt as he told of how he had prepared a hiding place in his backyard.

It was a hole in the ground, with a well-camouflaged cover. He, his wife, and their only daughter of twelve managed to stay hidden there throughout the first day of the "action." That night he climbed out, looked around, and decided it was a good time to escape. The problem was he could not convince his wife and his daughter. They were terrified about leaving the shelter. So he climbed back in and they made it through a second day of hiding. Outside they could hear much commotion, including many footsteps running in and out of their house and through the yard. Somebody was searching for them.

The second night the same thing happened again. Artsik climbed out but his wife and daughter again refused to leave the shelter. When the same scenario was repeated the third night, Artsik decided in desperation to strike out on his own and come back for them later with proof he had made it to the woods and back. But as things turned out, Artsik was never able to go back for them. He never knew how many days and nights they stayed in the hole before being discovered. And discovery was the only possible outcome.

Listening to the story, I was aware of the great pain and suffering Artsik was experiencing. He was weighed down with an enormous amount of guilt for having survived while his wife and daughter did not. Tormented with inner doubts and conflicts he alone knew, he was not the same man I'd known before the war—tall, erect, and full of life. Now he was a prematurely old man who walked with a stoop and was visibly broken, physically as well as spiritually. His face, wrinkled and folded, with deep shadowy pouches under his eyes, seemed to have fallen in, as though the scaffolding of bones that held it up had given way.

Artsik did not not survive the war. He was killed in May 1944. I saw him for the last time just two days before this happened. Various partisan brigades, exhausted by five weeks of continuous fighting, tried to break out of a German encirclement. Artsik didn't make it.

Eli Spektor—my sister Minya's brother-in-law— prepared a *malina* under the floorboards of a room in his house. He worked on it all through the summer of 1942. He had to be careful not to make any noise while constructing it and disposing of the debris, a task made more complicated by the fact that his house stood right next to the police station.

Then the "action" began. Present in Eli's house, besides his wife and two children, were also his sister-in-law, Tuaba Kaidanov, and their nephews, Jerry and Howard Kaidanov, and another sister-in-law, Feyge Gurevich, with her husband, Khaym-Zalman, and their two children, Hodl and Yakov. As they were getting into the *malina*, their neighbor Mendl Alperovits appeared seeking admittance for his daughter Freydl. "Not for myself," he kept on repeating, "just for my daughter. I am an old man. What could they possibly do to me?" He was known to be afflicted with spontaneous coughing fits and understood full well that had he himself asked to be admitted, he would have been a danger to everyone inside. The daughter was admitted. Then from their hiding place they all heard Mendl being beaten to death by the Germans, who wanted him to say where his daughter and neighbors were. The man did not reveal the information the Germans sought. All the people inside this *malina*, including Freydl, survived the war.

There is one more story to tell, this one about a young woman who successfully hid under the floor with her brother and their mother, but who had to leave her six-month-old baby outside in his crib in the room above them. They heard him being killed and could do nothing about it. They all came out the first night and reached the forest. The brother and sister survived the war, but the mother was killed in the summer of 1943, when the Germans attacked the forest and killed a number of Jews. Had they taken the baby into the hiding place, none of them would have survived.

Those were hard times and hard choices had to be made that exacted a terrible emotional toll. Some paid with their sanity. Others imposed upon themselves a crushing burden of guilt which to this day they have never been able to throw off.

Following the Kurenits "action," Vileyka had four ghettos: 1) the *Gebietskommissarsgetto* (provincial governor's ghetto), 2) the original ghetto in the two old Russian army barracks, 3) the SD ghetto, and 4) a commercial ghetto. This last had been created just two days earlier and consisted of four Kurenits families: Kantorovich, Kantor, Gershon Ejszyski, and Velvl Markman with his daughter Henya. Kantor was the son-in-law of the Kantoroviches.

These families had survived the Kurenits "action" in a *malina* and later reached the forest where most of the Kurenits Jews had taken refuge. Then, contrary to all logic, they bribed their way out of the woods and back into German hands and so-called German "protection." Life in the forest was not for them. They didn't like getting soaked through when it rained and they could not imagine surviving a winter there. Before the war they had been merchants in medicinal herbs and plants; they bought large quantities from the peasants and then shipped the stuff to various parts of Europe, where it was processed.

The Kantor family had two sons, the older of whom was Nyomke. He was about my age and I met him the day after his family arrived in Vileyka. He told me he wasn't happy about leaving the forest; he and his brother would have preferred to stay there but submitted to the decision to leave that their parents and grandparents made. He said he hoped to get back some day and told me what life was like there. It wasn't easy, he said, but it was certainly bearable. In this he contradicted the tales of woe his father was spreading. Where the older people found life in the forest intolerable, their children considered it challenging and adventuresome. Those of us who had been in the Vileyka ghetto since it was created, and especially the younger ones among us, thought that the Kantor family and the others had made a monumental mistake in exchanging the forest for the ghetto. A short time later their mistake proved fatal.

October 1942 came and with it a change in the prevailing weather; the air was now chilly and it often rained. Our spirits rose and fell according to whether the sun was shining or hidden. Rainy and cold weather brought with it a swell of dark and crushing depression and strengthened the position of those who, in our informal debates, advocated that we postpone our escape from the ghetto until the following spring. Then a fine sunny day would instill a new surge of hope and resolve in those of us who planned for an escape in the near future. Of course, none of us really had any idea at all of how to keep warm and dry in the woods and that realization tended to put a damper on even the most enthusiastic among us.

We also came to understand that the great majority of the ghetto residents were simply not ready to abandon "home," and that they were also adamant about preventing anyone else from leaving, thinking it would jeopardize the position of those who stayed behind. When this became clear to us, we knew that our organizing efforts had to go underground. From that time on, we communicated with each other secretly.

The plan for a substantial number of ghetto people to try and flee to the woods was doomed from the start and it remained doomed as long as one segment of the ghetto population, small as their numbers were, perceived that those who wished to depart constituted a serious threat to them. The words of one young tailor, a man in his thirties, still ring in my ears. The man had a wife and three children and he was absolutely determined to stay in the ghetto. He was one of its last inhabitants to be killed in July 1944, possibly just hours before the German retreat. This tailor was a timid soul, so I was all the more shocked to hear him, of all people, utter these words to me: "How much better off we'd be if you were dead!" That was no doubt the feeling of others, who thought they had to stay. I was a threat to them because they knew I was one of the organizers of a mass flight from the ghetto.

Our original plan of getting the entire ghetto, or at least a large part of it, out and into the woods would not work.

We would have only ourselves to look out for. Five of us, the hard core, were ready to go at any time. We were just waiting for final preparations to be completed and for the best time to be chosen. Another ten or twelve were undecided at that point. We stayed in constant contact with them and tried to sway them into coming with us.

This undecided group included the Spektor family, the head of which was Kopel Spektor, the locksmith I mentioned earlier in connection with the ammunition boxes. Kopel was about twenty-four years old. Before the war he had been a leader in the *Hashomer Hatsair* Zionist movement and he was one of the best volleyball players in Kurenits. He was also exceptionally intelligent and a wizard when it came to mechanics. He was the kind of person about whom people like to say, "That man has a good head on his shoulders." We younger people all looked up to him. The rest of his family consisted of his brother Eli, a young seventeen-year-old, and physically very strong, and two sisters, Sara-Feigl and Dina. Their parents had been killed in the Kurenits "action."

They also had an older sister, Ester, who was pretty, intelligent, and a teachers' college graduate. She had been living at home with their parents in Kurenits at the time of the "action," was spared, and then brought to the SD ghetto in Vileyka. After about two weeks an old medical problem flared up—tuberculosis of the knee—and she was admitted to the general hospital in Vileyka, where her two brothers and two sisters visited her regularly. Then one day, about a week after she had been admitted, they found her bed empty. It didn't take long to discover the bitter truth that the SD had taken her away and shot her.

As we analyzed it later, we decided that these tragic events may well have been the main factor in Kopel's eventual decision not to join us. We very much wanted his family to come. The sisters were welcome to come too, even though as a rule women were considered to be a handicap. Kopel's brother Eli wanted to come with us and maybe the sisters did too. I spoke with Kopel many times and pleaded with him to at least give his brother and sisters a chance, because they would never consent to leave without him. In the end he refused.

We now had ten people committed to leaving the ghetto. Simple as it may sound, leaving was actually a quite complicated undertaking. To begin with, you had to know where to go to find either partisans or at least fellow Jews who could initiate you into forest living. Knowing exactly where they could be located was essential. Otherwise, you could wander around for weeks without finding a safe place. With wet and cold weather at hand, it would be unwise to take that chance.

All through the summer, in the ghetto we'd heard stories about partisans in the woods. In reality, there were many different woods and very few partisans, and those few were constantly moving from one place to another, so running into partisans in the woods by chance was unlikely simply because the few partisans there were always on the move.

We also heard about what happened to the saddlers and our painter Yosef from Dolhinov, who lived with them. They had all actually left their house in Vileyka and made it to the woods, where they ran into many problems, all stemming from their ignorance about where to go once they got there. Their first piece of bad luck was starting off in the wrong direction; they went south towards the town of Molodechno, where the woods were too small to allow much, if any, movement by the partisans. Not knowing this, the group roamed the woods for four days and got wet and cold and hungry in the process. They also ran the risk of being denounced by the peasants they encountered all too often. Finally they gave up and came back to Vileyka. The Germans knew what had happened and accepted them back just the same, which isn't as odd as it may sound. To the Germans, it was a sort of propaganda victory. They counted on word of the saddlers' misadventure to spread quickly and discourage any desire that others might have to escape.

A further complication in undertaking a concerted escape attempt was that it would have to be done during the day, while we were at work. The larger the group, the more complicated this became because we were spread out all over town; different tradesmen worked at different jobs at different locations. So the signal for the escape had to be given ahead of time, in the morning, before we left for work and scattered.

On two separate occasions we actually gave the signal but had to call the escape off because somebody had gotten wind of our intentions and raised the alarm in the ghetto. The women of families chosing to stay, it turned out, were watching us like hawks. If we so much as dressed a little warmer than the weather seemed to call for, they decided something was up and ran to Schatz and informed on us. Harry Zimmerman and I were once called up in front of a high-ranking German official to take a slap and a tongue-lashing for trying to organize an escape. We denied it, of course. But somebody had obviously informed on us. This had a sobering effect. We became more secretive than ever. It was almost impossible, though, to avoid the constantly watching eyes of the ghetto women.

October of 1942 was drawing to a close; some mornings we would wake up and find frost on the ground. Unless we moved out soon, I thought, we'd be stuck here for good, or at least over the winter. Yet for one reason or another we weren't any closer to escaping than we had been a month earlier. We were simply unable, so it seemed, to follow a preconceived and organized plan. The escape, when it came, would have to be spontaneous. And for that, some sort of catalyst was required.

It came soon after in the form of a major tragedy on

November 7, which is the anniversary of the Russian revolution. Most of the time, the Germans picked a Jewish or Russian holiday on which to perform their terrible acts of murder. At about ten in the morning of November 7, a gentile woman who lived across the street from the old ghetto appeared at our ghetto with the terrible news that the entire population of the old ghetto had been wiped out during the night. She said they had been taken out to a small house in the woods about half a kilometer away. There, following the customary SD modus operandi, they were herded into the house and the house was set afire.

I happened to be in the workshop building when this news reached us and it caused an uproar. But already voices could be heard trying to question the validity of the news. "Don't listen to her. She only wants to upset us." "Don't listen to her. She must be an anti-Semite." The same old story all over again. People don't want to hear bad news and they mistrust and dislike the messenger who brings it.

I knew the woman by sight and may even have said hello to her sometimes when I lived in the old ghetto. She struck me as a decent person, certainly no anti-Semite. I also didn't believe for a moment that she had come to us with any intention other than to inform us of impending danger. The instant I heard the tragic news I knew it was true. I told the men right then and there that if it was true, we were going to leave that very day and that nothing—not even their informing on us—was going to hold us back. They argued that we had no way of verifying what had happened and it might take days to get a definite confirmation.

I brashly responded by volunteering to go up to the old ghetto and check the situation out personally. What I intended to do was get as close as I could and just observe the buildings for signs of life and activity. Normally, there would be women outside in the yard. Things would turn out quite differently.

I made it all the way to the last corner before the old ghetto without incident. Then as I turned the corner, about half a block from the first of the ghetto buildings, I came face to face with an SD guard. His presence there was proof enough the story was true. It also put me in mortal danger. The guard was patrolling the half-block area from the building to the street corner, back and forth, and it was my bad luck to run into him just as he was coming up to the corner. This gave me no chance whatever to back off—it would look like I was running away. And if the guard saw and thought that, he would surely shoot me.

I chose the only course of action I thought I had left: I acted as if I were just visiting and had no idea anything unusual had happened there during the night. I nonchalantly walked past the guard and went into the first building. The beds were unmade and there was absolutely no one there, no sign of life. The scene spoke for itself.

I called out the name of the ghetto leader several times, not expecting any reply, and of course none came. Now the hardest part. How was I to get out of there, past the guard, and around the corner, all in one piece? Frankly, I didn't expect to succeed.

I came out of the building. The guard was standing nearby, as if waiting for me, but his rifle was still slung over his shoulder. Maybe that's a good sign, I thought. Then I thought, but how long does it take to slide a rifle down into firing position? Only a second.

Walking neither fast nor slow I went by the guard and continued on towards the corner. This was certainly the longest and hardest half-block I have ever had to walk. It felt like ants were crawling up and down my spine. I expected to take a bullet at any moment.

Only when I had turned the corner did I relax a little and start breathing again. Yes, I was undoubtedly the only Jew to visit the old ghetto and see with his own eyes the absence of life there only hours after the residents' lives had been extinguished—the only Jew to do so and live to tell of it.

Ten minutes later I was back at the workshops and giving the people there the report of my harrowing experience. I told them what I had seen with my own eyes at the old ghetto. Now there could be no question about the truth of what the gentile woman had told us. Everybody had to believe it now. The Jews of the old ghetto were no longer among the living.

It was also obvious now that when the Germans had split the ghetto in two, they already had this outcome in mind. We didn't know it then, but found out after the war that the few Jews who lived in the commercial ghetto had also been liquidated that same night, possibly even in the same place.

I met with Yosef the painter and a few others we were close to and begged them to escape with us that same day.

"No," they said, "Not now. Wait until spring. Then we'll go with you."

Obviously, we weren't going to agree to that. We were going to escape that day, no matter what. Whoever wanted to come along was welcome. And on that note the meeting broke up.

Although people promised not to interfere with us, already ways were being found to discourage and delay us. My coat was snatched away and locked up in Schatz's office. How could I possibly leave in November without a coat, they must have figured. Well, they didn't count on our determination. That day I think I'd have left without any clothes at all.

There were sixteen of us ready and willing to go, all of us young and unmarried. Our plan was to walk through town singly or in pairs, staying at least one block apart. We would all dress as warmly as we could but we would wear our regular working clothes on top and carry tools of our trade. We would cross the railroad tracks at a little-used crossing and then regroup not far from the woods.

Our starting time was four in the afternoon. The day was cold but dry and we were grateful for that. By the time we joined together again the sun woud be setting and the Germans and the police were known to have a distaste for entering any woods after sundown, a fact we took into consideration.

I wanted to dress as warmly as I could, so I put on an extra pair of pants, a double shirt, and a wool sports jacket—all the clothes I owned. Unfortunately I had to leave behind the overcoat that had been locked up by those who wanted to dissuade me from going.

The fateful decision I took that Saturday in November saved my life.

Part II

The Partisan Underground

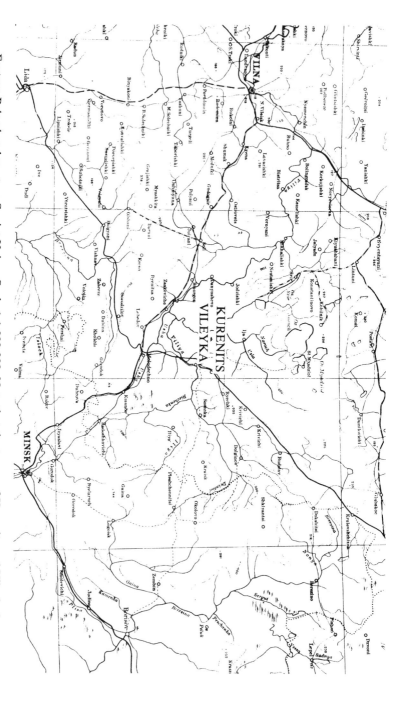

Eastern Poland and western Soviet Union. Scale 1:1,000,000. Note that the towns of Kurenits and Vileyka have been enlarged for easier identification, and do not represent their actual size. (Courtesy Map Collection, Yale University Library).

6

Thus began the exodus from Vileyka that was to save the lives of half of those in our group. We were leaving the ghetto on a journey into the unknown. We didn't know where our next meal was coming from, if we could keep warm with the few clothes we had on, or how we would cope with the danger and extreme discomfort that lay ahead. But despite all this, going held the hope of survival—an ingredient missing in the ghetto.

I can recall the names of only eight in our group: Tevl Kopolovits, Velvl the shoemaker, Khloyne and his brother Moyshe Leyzer Turov, Shimon Zimmerman and his girl friend (now his wife) Rivka Gordon, Leyka Alperovits, and a Vilno Jew by the name of Fima Levin. Of these eight only the last four survived.

None of us ran into any difficulty getting across town. We were dressed as if going to work. I carried two paint brushes and a wall-paint pattern. The others carried tools of their different trades.

We reassembled near the woods and counted all sixteen of us present: fourteen young men and two young women. Then we took off and discarded the yellow stars of David we had had to wear on our clothes at all times. The sun was quite low in the sky; it was less than half an hour to nightfall.

We took a small road into the woods that led in the general direction we were supposed to be going. One of our group, Leyka Alperovits, had a brother in the partisans. Leyka's brother had been able to get a message to her with instructions about where to go, the name of the village, and how to find the right house. We also had the name of a partisan contact, a woman we had known before the war as a Soviet activist.

We were all glad to be out of the confines of the ghetto and, more important, out of the hands of the Germans. Our immediate future might look clouded and full of uncertainties, but we were feeling, for the first time, a measure of freedom that just wasn't possible to experience in the ghetto. Yes, we were sure we had done the right thing in escaping and we were happy about it.

After some distance a second road crossed the one we were on and we didn't know which way to proceed. About a hundred meters further on, yet another road met the one we were on at a right angle. There stood a post with a number of road markers on it. I asked for two volunteers to come with me and check out the markers. That way we could orient ourselves properly. Velvl the shoemaker and Moyshe-Leyzer Turov the glazier responded. We walked to the intersection, read the road signs, and got our bearings. Then we turned back to join the others at the edge of the woods.

It was dusk by this time. There was still some faint light left in the open, but inside the woods it looked quite dark. To our surprise we found nobody back at the spot where we thought the group would be waiting for us. We searched for them for thirty meters in both directions. We even broke our rule of silence and called out, all to no avail. We were learning the first lesson in forest living. It's easy to get lost among the trees, especially after dark.

We had no choice but to keep going on our own. Moyshe-Leyzer Turov got quite upset about being separated from his brother Khloyne. We could only hope the rest of our group were going ahead too. It was fortunate we too had been privy to the information about how to reach the partisan contact. Without that, we might well have shared the fate of the Vileyka saddlers.

A few kilometers further on we realized we were hungry and decided to knock on the door of a house we were going by and ask for bread. The house was set back about fifty meters from the road and stood by itself, that is, it was isolated, not part of any village. A house like that was called a *khutor* (farmstead). The night was cold and dry and there was ample moonlight. We thought it more prudent for just one of us to go up to the house rather than all three of us together. So Moyshe-Leyzer and I stayed behind some bushes thirty meters away while Velvl went up and knocked on the door.

When the door opened, a man about thirty years old stepped outside. He had a long knife in his hand. The steel glittered in the moonlight. He walked towards Velvl, who, scared out of his wits, kept retreating at the same pace. For a moment it looked as if they were both doing some ritual dance in the moonlight. Then the man's arm holding the knife began to move upwards in an arc.

"Bread you want? I'll give you this instead!"

With that, both of us behind the bushes came out and started moving towards Velvl. In my hands I held a long stick I had picked up several kilometers back as a defense against dogs. I hoped that the sight of two more people, one carrying something perhaps resembling a rifle, might stop the man.

It worked. Seeing us approach, he cut short his attack,

and went back inside the house, mumbling something like "I have no bread."

We were all shaken, especially Velvl. Maybe the man was a policeman. Without our intervention, Velvl would have been a dead man.

Later, when I became a partisan, I often thought about that incident. It rankled me and I regretted I could not have settled the score with that man. But I was stationed over a hundred kilometers away and throughout the war I never got much closer to him. Even to this day I feel a twinge that he got away scot-free.

We kept on walking for another hour. Hunger convinced us to try our luck at another house. This time an older woman opened the door. She brought out a large loaf of black bread weighing about three kilos. She cut off a third for herself and gave us the rest.

Fortified by a sizable chunk of the bread, we continued on our way. But we soon felt tired and in need of rest. Leaving the road, we went a short way into the woods that lined both sides of the road. We lay down on the ground, which was covered with dry pine needles. We were overheated from all that marching and didn't feel the night cold. After a while we felt rested, got up, and resumed our journey.

Around midnight we came to the village and found the right house; the woman opened the door and let us in. She let us rest for a couple of hours and then instructed us to go on to another village about two kilometers further on. She told us how to find the house of the local shoemaker there. Jews from the forest, she said, often stopped by that house before dawn on their way back from collecting food at night.

We found the village and the house easily; it was the only house with light showing through the windows. We knocked at the door and were let in. The shoemaker was already up and at work.

We were quite happy to find a Jew from Kurenits there, Iche Fiedler. Until then we didn't know he had survived. He told us his wife Khana and their son Mendl, about eleven then, also survived. Their older daughter Mina had died in the Purim "action" in Vileyka. Their younger daughter Sarah had been killed by lightning before the war, in 1940. Of course Iche was quite surprised to see us, too, as he obviously had no idea we had escaped from Vileyka.

The village was right on the edge of the forest. Jews felt somewhat safer lingering here than in more distant villages they visited to beg for food. Iche opened the large canvas bag he had with him to show us what he had collected that night. There were about eight or ten pieces of bread weighing more or less a kilo each, a bottle of milk, and a few pieces of hard cheese. He usually walked all night, he said, going through several villages, knocking on doors and asking for food. Once in a while he would get lucky and be given a piece of butter or some cereals and beans for a soup. It was quite rare to get a piece of meat. Not every house he stopped at had enough food to give any away and others didn't feel like giving. Usually, though, such a night of collecting would bring in enough food to last a family several days. Then the process was repeated, this time selecting different villages in order not to overburden the same households too often.

Close to 200 people lived in the forest, he said, and they all gathered food the same way. On any given night, it was not unusual to find thirty to forty men and women in small groups of two or three busily collecting food in villages inside the forest and up to ten kilometers from it. Since the enterprise was spontaneous and uncoordinated, some villages or individual houses were approached too often and this unquestionably caused resentment among the villagers. This bad feeling may have had something to do with the attacks the Germans and the police subsequently made on

Jewish survivors in the forest, attacks that resulted in many casualties.

Iche Fiedler named most of the survivors living in the forest. These were people we knew, of course, but whose fate had not been known to us.

We spent about an hour waiting for daylight, at which time we would enter the forest and go to the campsite. To pass the time, I watched the shoemaker doing his work by the light of a *luchina* (peasant torch), a strip of wood from a pine log that resembles a wooden yardstick in almost every dimension. As a child, before the war, I had heard that while kerosene lamps were beginning to be widely adopted, the *luchina* remained the most common source of light for most villagers. It became even more common during the war, of course, when kerosene was hard to come by. But this was the first time I had actually seen one.

A *luchina* gave off a meager light, about as much as two candles, and smoked considerably more, depending on the amount of resin a particular strip of wood contained. The unlit end was stuck into a special niche in the wall. If angled properly, it would burn uninterruptedly for about five to seven minutes. The most suitable sections of logs were cut from pine, about a meter long, and free of knots so the thin strips would split off evenly and easily. For the next year and three-quarters, that is, until the Red Army drove the Germans out in July 1944, the *luchina* was our main means of illumination, and I became quite good at making them.

The shoemaker was working on a pair of *laptyes* (bast shoes). This was a type of footwear worn by most villagers in our part of the country before the war because leather shoes or boots were too expensive and beyond the means of many of the peasants. A *laptye* had a high canvas upper that reached halfway up to the knees. It was held in place with lacings of rope or strips of hide. For the sole, people used a piece of leather or a section of an old discarded automobile tire. If made well, they were attractive and comfortable to wear.

As I sat waiting, my thoughts wandered back to the ghetto we had left barely fourteen hours earlier. From the moment I took that first step towards freedom I never regretted my decision. Instinctively, I knew it was the right thing to do. I was happy to have reached the safety of the forest, but I was also somewhat uneasy about the possible consequences of our flight on those we had left behind. Would they be punished in some way, or would their lives continue as before? I had no answers to these questions until the liberation and my return to Kurenits in August 1944, because I stayed only a short while in the Katlovtse forest, where most of the Kurenits Jews took refuge. Those who did remain managed to get sketchy information about what was going on in the Vileyka ghetto. Sometimes a peasant would be able to take a brief note to the ghetto and bring back a reply, a risky service for which the messenger was paid handsomely. Thus, some contact was maintained with the ghetto. Even though this contact can be credited with saving the lives of a few, it was also directly responsible, inadvertently, for the death of most of the Vileyka ghetto Jews.

Four months after we escaped, a great calamity befell the Vileyka ghetto. The Germans did not plan it and neither they nor the Jews expected it. It came about as a result of people misinterpreting a small and insigificant incident, which set off a chain of events which, once started, could not be stopped until the whole drama was played out to its terrible conclusion.

As it turned out, the Germans did not retaliate for our escape from the ghetto in any way. The lives of the ghetto residents went on approximately as they had before we escaped—until the eighteenth of March 1943.

A peasant drove by the ghetto in a horse-drawn wagon

and handed a letter from the forest people to one of the women standing there. At any hour of the day, ghetto women were usually out at the fence, looking longingly towards the rest of the town and watching the people and traffic moving freely there—not unlike prisoners on death row who look out through the barred windows of their cells at the free movement in the street outside, though the women were less likely to get a reprieve. The peasant said he would be back in an hour to pick up a letter of reply.

He reappeared when he said he would and was handed the letter of reply. The women watched him drive off and were glad that everything seemed to have gone off smoothly. But about a block away they saw, to their horror, a policeman stop the horse and wagon, talk briefly to the peasant, and then get on the wagon and drive away with the peasant. Nothing like this had ever happened before. What could it mean? The women concluded that the peasant had been arrested.

They then let their imaginations run wild and concluded further that the police had known all along what the peasant was doing and had just been waiting to pounce on him when the time was right. Surely, the women figured, the letter would be found on the peasant and serve as conclusive proof that the ghetto was in contact with the forest people, which the Germans would interpret as conclusive proof of contact with the partisans. Then someone said they had heard that ammunition had been placed in the wagon for delivery to the forest. Apparently, some ghetto residents had secretly continued to supply the partisans with the ammunition from the attic of the theater, an undertaking I had initiated in the summer of 1942. The same peasant who acted as messenger between the forest Jews and the ghetto also brought out the ammunition, usually stacked in hollowed-out boards. It was not hard for people to visualize where the discovery of the letter and the ammunition would lead. The women foresaw the most terrible consequences for the ghetto residents.

How could the women know that all of their conjectures were without basis in fact and sprang only from fertile imaginations, excited by the stressful situation? In fact, the scene the women observed was mundane, but only the forest people would know it. When the peasant delivered the letter of reply to the proper forest person, he mentioned that near the ghetto a policeman had asked him for a short lift. But the tragedy had already begun to play itself out, swiftly and terribly, as if its fury were guided and directed by the invisible hand of Satan.

The women who had just seen the policeman climb onto the peasant wagon ran crying and moaning in full panic into the workshops and notified the men of what they were sure had happened. Pandemonium broke loose. People expected the Germans to come at any moment and shoot everyone. Only one course of action lay open. They must make a run for it, try and escape. So run for their lives they did with no time to lose and without stopping for extra clothes or food. Disorganized and panicked, they grabbed their children and ran off into the direction of the old ghetto, completely logical in that it was the shortest way to the woods, which lay just a kilometer away.

The Germans seemed to have been prepared for such an eventuality and were waiting for the fleeing Jews at several strategic spots they would have to negotiate. One of these was the railroad crossing and it was there the massacre began.

There was still an hour or two of daylight left. The SD troops picked the escapees off with rifle and machine gun fire like ducks in a shooting gallery. Some of the escapees got across the tracks somehow; others were driven back time and time again by the heavy gunfire. The impact of the bullets tore babies from the arms of their parents. People were dropping left and right. Some were only wounded but there was no way their family members could get to them and help them.

Some families were wiped out completely, while others came through completely unscathed. Still others had partial losses. Kopel Spektor and his brother Eli, who had decided not to come away with us, were both killed. So was their sister Sara-Feigl. Only their younger sister Dinka got through, though wounded in the leg; luckily for her the wound was only superficial and she was able to get to the forest with other survivors. Today she resides in Israel.

The tragedy was compounded in the case of the sisters Leyka and Libe, who had been neighbors of mine in Kurenits before the war and lived in the ghetto with their husbands. Both families had little boys the same age—about two and a half. The older sister also had an older boy, about ten or eleven years old. When the shooting stopped and the survivors could take stock of their losses, three of the seven members in these two families were dead. Leyka survived, but her son was torn from her arms by bullets. Her husband was also killed; he was left lying somewhere near the railroad tracks. Libe was killed but her two sons and her husband survived.

Velvl Rabunski, his wife Rosa, and their young son of three, together with several stragglers who joined them, stayed hidden for twenty-six hours until things quieted down and they were able to make it across the tracks. The same gentile woman who came to the ghetto on November 7, 1942, to warn us about the liquidation of the old ghetto, gave Velvl food for the children in his group and pointed out a hiding place for them at a time when the whole area was swarming with Germans and police.

As Velvl Rabunski told me later, there were a hundred and twenty-six people in the ghetto before the tragic events of March 18, 1943. A few families did not take part in the attempted escape, some because they were old, others because they decided they would be better off staying put in the ghetto. Approximately thirty people in all stayed behind. Less than a third of the escapees made it through. Only twenty-four reached Katlovtse forest and survived the war. The rest were all massacred during the escape. The thirty who stayed behind were kept alive by the Germans until the last day or so of the German occupation when they were liquidated perhaps just a few hours before the Red Army reached Vileyka.

Shimon Zimmerman, who was a member of a partisan group operating near Kurenits and Vileyka when that area was liberated in the summer of 1944, entered Vileyka within a day after its liberation. (He was a member of the group of sixteen who escaped with me from the Vileyka ghetto on November 7, 1942.) Shimon went through the ghetto and the workshops and discovered a note placed conspicuously under a large plane. The note had been left there by Motke (Abes) the carpenter. It was written in Yiddish and said: "All of us are alive at this date" (and gave the date). "We can hear heavy guns in the distance and the rumble of German tanks retreating. We know the liberation of Vileyka is near at hand. We also know we are not going to survive."

I was familiar with the thinking of the different groups in the ghetto up to the time I left it and I knew to what lengths some people were ready to go in order to keep others from leaving. It is safe to assume that even if the events of March 18, 1943, had not taken place, the fate of all 126 remaining residents of the ghetto would have been the same as the thirty who stayed behind. It would never have been possible to organize a mass escape, what with one delay after another and the constant surveillance of those unwilling to leave. Looked at in this light, the events of March 18 were still tragic for the twenty-four who successfully escaped, but without those events the twenty-four would almost surely not have survived.

I could see the first gray of dawn begin to show through the shoemaker's window. It was time for us to take leave of the shoemaker and his hospitality and go into the forest. Iche had advised us to wait for morning light because the camp-site was about four kilometers inside the forest and in the dark people might not see the trail and get lost. We started out.

Before long we reached the camp and met many of the survivors. They were spread out over an area of about three square kilometers. Each family gathered around its own fire. Sometimes the remnants of two or more families came together as one unit around a single fire. A unit like that was more viable than the individual parts would have been on their own. Some families had found their niches several kilometers away, apart from the main body. I heard about them but never got to see them in the short time I stayed in the forest.

People were already digging bunker-like winter homes, I was told. Eventually the great majority built underground shelters. Nonetheless, some families spent the whole win-ter above ground, no small feat considering the harshness of Russian winters in general and the exceptional cold of that winter in particular. Only the fire they kept burning continuously kept them from freezing.

I was welcomed to the fire of Eli Spektor, the brother of Sam Spektor, my brother-in-law, and I stayed with them for about a week. I then spent a few nights with newfound friends with whom I would shortly leave Katlovtse forest for another location. In all, I was in the forest for about ten days.

The two companions who arrived with me were taken in by other families. Young and healthy people were wel-come to stay with almost any family because they could help in the necessary tasks of collecting food, cutting and gathering wood for the fire, and so on.

At our fire, there were—besides Eli, his wife Rokhl and their two children—Tauba Kaidanov, Eli's sister-in-law, from the town of Krivich, the Spektors' nephews Jerry

Kaidanov, a lad of about ten, and his older brother Howard, age twelve, and Freydl Alperovits.

I was told that Jerry had adapted himself quite well to forest living. He knew every road, path, and trail and could find his way anywhere, even in the dark, no small feat for one so young. During the warmer seasons, partisan groups that were temporarily stationed in the forest, or just passing through, often used Jerry as a guide.

All of these people at Eli Spektor's fire had hidden together in the same *malina* in Kurenits and they stayed together in the woods. We all slept on pine branches spread in a circle around the fire. "Slept," in the sense of getting a restful night's sleep, is not the right word. The side exposed to the fire would get unbearably hot within minutes, while the side away from the fire came close to freezing. This made us doubly uncomfortable and we were obliged to turn over every five minutes or so. It was also not unusual to wake up and find our clothes smoldering, or even on fire, from the exploding sparks that burning wood especially pine, produces. Under these conditions, real sleep of any length was quite impossible.

I spent my first day in the forest walking around through the camp and stopping to visit with people at the various fires. I heard details about the Kurenits "action" from eyewitnesses—most of the people in the Katlovtse forest were survivors from Kurenits, although a few families from other towns had also found their way here.

Many people went for days, even weeks, without so much as a rudimentary wash. I remember I had to force myself to shave and wash my face with ice water in the cold of winter. I particularly remember one family from the town of Varnyan. What makes them stand out in my memory is the way they bathed their youngest daughter, who was about one or one-and-a-half years old. They would undress her completely and wash her in cold water. The baby hardly complained. Though it was difficult, and at times pure agony, to keep up even a semblance of good hygiene, yet here was this little girl, stark naked in the freezing weather, being washed with ice-cold water and making hardly a whimper. I was afraid she would come down with pneumonia any day. Miraculously, she not only survived but thrived in the harsh conditions in the woods. When I ran into the family again, in a West German displaced persons camp in 1946, I was pleasantly surprised to see before me a beautiful round-faced, rosy-cheeked five-year-old girl, the healthiest of the lot; here was the same child I had seen in the woods.

The first night after our arrival from the ghetto I went out with Eli and one other person to collect food. They were both old hands at it and knew all the roads and tracks, all the ins and outs of the woods. They knew which houses to approach and which to avoid. I believe we covered some ten or twelve kilometers and three villages while out collecting.

The Germans and the police rarely visited these villages, but partisans did so occasionally, and forest Jews quite often. No doubt some villagers gave food to the Jews out of compassion. Most, however, gave out of a desire for self-preservation. They didn't want to offend either the authorities, the partisans, or the Jews, whom they assumed to be under partisan protection. The partisans had a fierce reputation because they had no compunction about burning down the houses of those they suspected of supplying information to the enemy or even executing these informers.

The true state of affairs between partisans and forest Jews was somewhat different, however. When partisans were present in the forest they would sometimes help feed the Jews, but their concern for the welfare of the forest Jews hardly ever went beyond that. And most of the time there were no partisans around. In particular there was no partisan group in the forest that entire winter. But the myth of partisan protection certainly helped the forest Jews and the Jews did what they could to foster it. It was no secret that the majority of villagers considered the Jews at best pests and at worst a considerable burden, because feeding the forest survivors during the two years they were in the forest fell on the shoulders of the same villages and households in the area.

Collecting food from reluctant villagers was one of the main problems the forest inhabitants faced and it was one of the principal reasons I decided to leave the area as soon as I could. Sooner or later the Germans and the police would find out there were no partisans in these woods, after which they would no longer be averse to entering and attacking the Jews, which is eventually what happened in the Katlovtse forest. The Jews were attacked twice and a considerable number were killed, including three of the original sixteen that had left the ghetto with me.

As Velvl Rabunski later recounted to me, the first attack took place on May 1, 1943. The second, which caused much heavier casualties, came in September 1943 and lasted for two weeks. About a third of the forest inhabitants lost their lives in the course of these two attacks. The two-thirds who survived owe their lives to the vastness of the forest and, most likely, to the small and inadequate body of troops and police sent in to get them. Many forest Jews camouflaged themselves on the ground or under branches and were passed over unnoticed. Others were pursued all over the forest but managed to stay one step ahead of their pursuers, who eventually gave up.

The second day after my arrival at the camp I was introduced to a family from Postov consisting of a mother, her twenty-year-old daughter, the daughter's fiancé, and the woman's son, Mulke Zaslavsky, who was a partisan and just back visiting together with a friend of his, also a partisan. The two partisans were both armed with rifles and grenades and my eyes popped when I saw them. These were the first partisans I had ever laid eyes on and one of them was even a Jew. All the time I was in the ghetto my dream had been to be armed the way these men were and become a partisan to fight the Germans. Regrettably, the two men could not help me make my dream come true. I had to be satisfied with just holding the rifle for a while and being shown how to work the lock and aim it.

The pair belonged to a partisan unit stationed to the east, that is, to the east of the old Polish-Russian border before the war. (Similarly, we called everything "west" that was west of the old pre-war border and belonged to Poland.) They were en route to or from some special assignment and managed to spend a couple of days with the Zaslavsky family in the forest.

While I was talking with them, a Kurenits survivor came up and told them about a peasant who had been given two cows for safekeeping by a Jew who was subsequently killed in the Kurenits "action." The man asked the two partisans to help him get the two cows back and bring them into the forest. The partisans agreed and then asked me if I wanted to come along. I readily accepted.

The village the peasant lived in was about ten kilometers away and just five kilometers from Kurenits. It was considered German territory during the day; at night, however, partisans roamed at will there and even much closer to Kurenits, where a sizable police force was garrisoned. We encountered no problems in getting the cows back. I noticed that people didn't argue too much with armed partisans. We got back, dog-tired but happy, just as the sun was coming up. The entire camp feasted on meat for the next several days.

A couple of days later I met a small group of young people from the town of Dokshits. They were Idl Jyesin, Shaya Sussman, his sister Khaya Ester Sussman, and Motl Varfman. With them also was Rivka Melamed from Dolhinov, who was Khaya Ester's sister-in-law. As we talked it seemed like we were all in agreement about the shortcomings of our present location so far as safety was concerned. Slowly the idea emerged of going somewhere else for the winter, to a place where our presence would not be common knowledge to all the local villagers. We decided to go north to a wooded area on the other side of the town of Dokshits, about fifty kilometers from where we then were. Idl was quite familiar with the woods there and knew every village, road, and track in the area. Our plan was to reach the woods, find a suitable place, and build a *zemlyanka* (dugout or underground shelter). We would then stock the shelter with enough food to last us the winter. Soon two more young men joined our group: Hershl Zimmerman, who had escaped from the ghetto with me, and a barber from the town of Krasne.

We began making preparations for the trip. What we needed most was enough food to last us for at least a week until we had settled in at the new place and had got a feel of the area. The next night four of us set out towards a distant village that was not frequented by the forest people because it was so far away and also because there was a police garrison nearby.

In our group, Motl owned a sawed-off rifle, a sorry piece of armament. The trigger mechanism did not work, but, he assured us, it could be made to go off by hitting the gun-lock hard. Given this condition, it was of course out of the question to aim the weapon. Motl had only three rounds of ammunition to go with his rifle, so we couldn't test it anyway. In the end, when we did have to use it, it didn't work at all. We couldn't even get a bang out of it to scare off a menacing dog.

Another man in our group had fashioned what could pass for a revolver from a tree root. He carried it in a leather holster and it looked authentic enough, especially at night.

These two pieces of "firepower" were supposed to make believe our claims that we were partisans. We had no difficulty getting enough bread and meat for the trip we planned. We also borrowed a horse and sleigh from a peasant to bring our supplies in close to the forest. At the edge of the forest, we turned the horse around and gave it a pat to send it on its way back with the sleigh to find its master. Horses have an uncanny knack of being able to find their way home and will do so unerringly almost all the time. I remember how impressed I had been with stories about how disputes over the rightful ownership of a horse were settled by letting the horse loose and seeing where it went. A horse would find its way back home even after an absence of two years or more.

While we were in the village where we got our supplies I noticed another village about a kilometer away and out of curiosity asked what its name was. Uzentse, I was told. That struck a sentimental chord. My father had been born and raised there and his family lived there for many years. I looked at the houses silhouetted against the night sky with some emotion and wondered if maybe I was seeing the house my father was born in. How I would have loved to visit the village and talk with old-timers who might remember my father or my grandparents. I felt the pull of my roots. But this was not to be. Several policemen lived in Uzentse and it was unsafe to enter, even at night, let alone during the day. Besides, my interest was strictly personal and my friends wouldn't share it. Yet I had heard the name of Uzentse village mentioned so many times while I was growing up that it had taken on a special, almost mystical, meaning for me. Now I had to be satisfied with just looking at it from a distance and at night, knowing this was as close as I would probably ever get.

One afternoon, after our preparations were all complete,

we set out on our journey. Idl acted as our navigator. In one village, some distance from the forest, we persuaded a peasant to hitch up his horse and sleigh and give us a lift. After thirty kilometers or so we dismissed him and picked up another driver with horse and sleigh for the second part of the trip. This driver was nosy. He looked us over, his eyes darting from the rifle to the revolver and then over those of us without arms. He wondered aloud why the rest of us weren't armed. The excuse we gave him may not have allayed his suspicions but the presence of the arms we did have kept him in line. What he didn't know or suspect, so far as I could see, was that our rifle wouldn't fire and our revolver was a fake.

The closer we got to the area we planned to settle in, the more shaky our original plan became. We had counted on finding an area free of the enemy as well as of partisans. Instead, the further north we drove, the more partisans we ran into. At first we were glad, hoping they would let us join up with them. It was mere wishful thinking; none would accept us.

We finally stopped at a village called Charnitse, where a whole *otryad* (company) of partisans were stationed. I was impressed at seeing how the partisans moved around freely in and between the villages during the day and how they were stationed in one village over a long period of time. The area around this place was obviously much more secure than the area around Katlovtse forest, where this sort of thing would not have been possible in December 1942.

Having grown up in town, I found the arrangements out here in the country quite Spartan, little more than the bare necessities. The house of the family I stayed with in Charnitse was typical of the village and the region, consisting of a single large room, about seven by seven meters in size. Each corner of the room held its own distinctive furniture.

In one corner stood a massive clay oven that took up half the length of the wall. The oven was used year-round for cooking and baking, and in winter the top of the oven served as a warm and cozy place to sleep. The real bed was set up in the next corner, which was little more than some planks laid across two wooden trestles, and a straw mattress laid out on top of the planks. The corner diagonally across from the oven was the dining area, with a wooden table and benches. The last corner, coming around to the oven again, was a utility area, with some shelves and a spinning wheel. A storage area was located out in an entrance-shed attached to the one-room house, and here were kept the farming tools and wood for the oven. Food that might be damaged by frost—potatoes, mostly—was kept inside, often under the trestle bed.

The floor inside the house was the earth itself, hardened by long use to the consistency of concrete. I slept on this earthen floor in front of the oven, with some straw underneath me for softness and insulation, and a bundle of straw for a pillow. It seemed the height of luxury, coming after the nights out in the open in Katlovtse forest. I could once more sleep the whole the night through without tossing and turning and waking.

Our first day in Charnitse, we met Zelig Telis, a young Jewish member of the Dubrov partisan brigade, stationed farther to the east. He was on temporary duty, as liaison officer with the Medvedov partisan brigade, stationed here in Charnitse. Zelig was a native of the town of Dokshits and knew or was acquainted with most of the members of our little band. We told him that our main objective was to join the partisans and we asked him to put in a good word for us with the officer-in-charge. He did, and we were provisionally accepted, on the condition that we furnish our own weapons.

At first this seemed unreasonable. How on earth were

we going to come by firearms, I wondered, and where? Eventually I learned that practically all partisan brigades then willing to take on recruits required them to join with their own weapons. The reasons were twofold. First, the partisans were themselves desperately short of weapons and had none to issue to recruits, and second, the partisans thought the requirement would encourage the recruits to scrounge around and bring to light some of the vast stores of arms and ammunition that the Red Army had abandoned in the confusion of its retreat. Some of these abandoned arms and ammunition were known to have been left in depots and warehouses; others, abandoned by individual Russian soldiers in the field to lighten their loads and make escape easier, were believed to have been discovered and hidden by peasants. This included both light weapons—like rifles, ammunition, and hand grenades—and, occasionally, machine guns and submachine guns. Potential recruits might already have a line on some of the hidden weapons or be motivated to develop leads. But Motl Varfman and I, despite our efforts, could find no weapons, nor could several others.

As a result, we were not allowed to join the partisans, so we decided to move farther east, to the other side of the old Polish-Russian border, where, people said, there were many more resistance group. There, we thought, we would be more likely to find a brigade willing to take us in even though we didn't have our own weapons.

Motl's foot was sore from our long walks to Dokshits in search of weapons and he needed a day or so to recuperate. The barber and Harry were anxious to take off at once and left the next day. I didn't want to leave Motl behind, so I decided to stay on with him until he was ready to travel.

Motl and I set out a day later, and for the next two weeks we kept finding we'd taken the same route that the barber and Harry had. The barber cut a distinctive figure. He was a tall man and he wore a Red Army hat. In every village we came through, we'd ask after them and the answer was always that, yes, they certainly had been noticed, and then people went on to describe the tall man with the conspicuous Red Army hat. But even though we kept track of them as we moved east, we never quite caught up. Eventually, all of us wound up in the Ushachi region but in separate partisan brigades.

The barber didn't survive the war. He was killed in a skirmish with the Germans. Harry did survive, but I didn't see him again until May 1944. The unit he was with had spent three weeks in swampland surrounded by Germans. When what was left of his unit finally broke out, they came to the village where my unit was staying. I remember being shocked by his appearance. The rags he wore for clothes hung in tatters. He was going barefoot because, as he told me, his boots had rotted away in the dampness of the swamp. All the exposed parts of his body—especially his face, arms, and legs—were bloody and swollen from mosquito bites. In short, he looked like a pack of dogs had mauled him and then left him for dead. But he was alive and that was what was important.

As Motl and I continued eastward, we entered into a corridor of territory under partisan control. There we could go through villages in broad daylight and keep on walking as long as there was light to see by. Because this was partisan country, neither the Germans nor the police dared set foot in it. Later, we found out that this corridor was a full hundred kilometers in length—extending all the way to the city of Polotsk—and about forty kilometers wide. It was almost like a separate state; the partisans even collected taxes from the peasants in the form of food and clothing.

When Motl and I were hungry we'd stop at a village and knock on doors until we found a place where the people had food they were willing to share with us. The inhabitants were usually as generous as they could be. They knew they had to feed the partisans and the few civilians that passed through. We also usually managed to get put up for the night without too much trouble.

I couldn't help noticing how much worse off most villagers were here in the east compared with villagers on the western side of the old Polish-Russian border, who had only lived under Russian rule for less than two years. In the west there was food to be had even during the war; here in the east food was truly in short supply. But maybe it was because these folks in the east understood hunger that they were willing to share what they had with us. Several times I remember having difficulty swallowing the bread we were offered, the same bread they were eating. It looked all right but tasted terrible. The flour it was made from had been "extended" with chaff and other unnourishing fillers, the sort of thing that usually went to the pigs and cattle. Nowadays, as one woman put it, they used to make the bread "go a little further."

Each day we would run into small groups of partisans on the road, going to or coming from special tasks they had been sent to perform. They told us of larger partisans units further to the east, even garrisons and permanent stations. So we kept on heading east.

We reached the town of Ushachi. Before the war it had counted about 8,000 inhabitants and had been the seat of county administration. Now the population was down to about a third of what it had been. Many houses were abandoned and empty; other houses were occupied by elderly people and middle-aged women with children. Most men of military age had retreated with the Russians, while most of the others had left to join the partisans. There was something depressing about Ushachi. I remember feeling this not only on the first time I was there but each time I came back during the year and a half I was in the region as a partisan. I never stayed overnight in Ushachi or even stopped long enough to have a meal. The atmosphere was different from what it was in the smaller villages, where most people were more pleasant and friendly.

We were now in the dead of winter. Sometimes, the weather was so bad that Motl and I had no choice but to stay on in some village and wait it out. Other times we'd get caught on the road between villages by an unexpectedly heavy snowfall or, worse, by a mixture of snow and sleet that the howling wind would blow horizontally into our faces and eyes. By contrast, I loved to travel on foot when weather was dry and cold and sunny. The perfect stillness would then be broken only by the crunch of our footsteps in the snow. And how clean and bright the snow was that spread out in every direction as far as we could see! It sparkled as if an invisible giant hand had lavishly sprinkled diamonds all over the surface. Sometimes the temperature dropped as low as 35 degrees Celsius below freezing. That was when I remembered and silently thanked the partisan in Charnitse who'd given me his old sheepskin coat. I'd have been in real trouble without it.

The soles of my boots were beginning to wear thin and before long they were in urgent need of repair. I still carried half of a large piece of hard sole leather that Harry and I had brought all the way from the Vileyka ghetto and that we divided in two before we went our separate ways in Charnitse. In one of the villages I found a young shoemaker who was able to resole my boots with the piece of hard leather. In appreciation, I left him what remained of it, a piece large enough for another pair of soles.

Two weeks into our trek eastward from village to village, Motl and I overtook a group of about forty refugees, some from my hometown of Kurenits. They were under the charge of two partisans who had been entrusted by their commanding officer with the task of escorting the refugees eastward to the front.

The group had started out in the region of the Katlovtse

forest in October 1942, about three months earlier. The part of the front they were headed to was far to the northeast, between the cities of Velikie Luki and Tarapets, over 600 kilometers away as the crow flies, but three times that distance in actual trekking. There, with the help of Red Army personnel, they hoped to get through the German positions and into Russian-held territory, whence they would then be evacuated to the rear and beyond. At least that was the way it was explained to me, and when I first heard about it I was skeptical. How on earth could a group of civilians, most of whom were women, and some pretty old at that, led by only two partisans, make it through almost 2,000 kilometers of enemy territory? They'd have to ford several rivers and cross two or three railroad lines that the Germans guarded closely. But the most incomprehensible part for me was how anybody could possibly get through the front line.

I suppose I was thinking of stories I'd heard and films I'd seen that depicted conditions the way they were in World War One, a well-defined line set off with trenches and foxholes, with bunkers and machine gun nests here and there on either side of a no-man's-land that even a rat would have a hard time getting across alive. Yet here was this group of mostly unarmed civilians apparently proposing to do just that.

After a little explaining, backed up by the testimony of several local partisans I met, the incomprehensible became comprehensible and even obvious. Groups had been crossing the front line for the better part of a year, usually with a high degree of success, and the enterprise had the blessing and backing of the Russians. This route to safety was practicable, but long, tortuous, and extremely dangerous. However, a great many people had taken it and gotten through. For instance, Harry Zimmerman's parents, their son Judl—my erstwhile fellow painter back in Vileyka—their niece Beatrice, and her father had made it into Russia this way and there they spent the remainder of the war. After the war, I met many others who had taken the same route.

It worked like this. All the way to the front the route was sprinkled with pockets under partisan control. A group of refugees headed for the front would move from one pocket to the next, supported by the food and protection local villagers and partisans gave them. Crossing the front line was not as complicated as I had imagined, either. This war was being fought under strategic concepts different from those of World War One. When there was no fighting going on, the front line consisted of fortified garrisons situated about one kilometer or more apart from each other. A small group of refugees could slip through between them, provided they had someone to guide them through the minefields. And that's where Red Army personnel came in. They had the expertise and experience to do such things.

Movement through the front line was also one of the most important ways of supplying the partisans with arms and ammunition. A partisan who got across to the Russian side would, after a chance to rest, be loaded up with several rifles or machine guns and as much ammunition as one person could carry and then dispatched back to his unit of origin, sometimes a thousand kilometers or more away.

What was even more remarkable was that all these partisans, and the civilians they escorted—often members of their own families, and sometimes Jews—used exactly the same route of roads and trails, including river and railroad crossings, as the groups that preceded and followed them and that this had been going on for almost a whole year. Hundreds of partisan groups had taken the same route. A single village on the banks of the Dvina River served as the "jumping-off place" for getting across the river.

Getting to the front and across it was no easy undertaking. The distance that had to be traveled, on foot, could amount to two thousand kilometers or more, depending on the number and length of the detours that were necessary to avoid enemy garrisons or unexpected enemy forces. Such distances could be very taxing, especially for older people. In addition, some of the groups were attacked along the way, the unlucky ones more than once, and some groups took casualties. Despite all these difficulties and hazards, this was the route many Jews took. The great majority of them made it through and survived, and, after the war, eventually resurfaced in the West.

After the war I met several families who had made journeys like this and they described to me some of the hardships and difficulties they had encountered. Some of them had spent four months on the road covering great distances before getting through the front line, all of it on foot. Much of the time they had to walk at night and stop when daylight made it unsafe to go on. Only in the pockets of partisan territory did they feel secure enough to sleep at night and walk during the day. And getting to the other side of the front line did not necessarily bring an end to their ordeal. When they were put on trains, to be evacuated far to the rear, thousands of kilometers away, they were often subjected to aerial bombardments and once more they suffered casualties.

In 1946 I met one family, from the town of Krivich, that had been on one of these treks "beyond the front line," as they were called at the time. The family consisted of both parents and two sons, ages sixteen and twelve, and even though they all survived, they were nevertheless touched by tragedy on the journey.

One evening, at dusk, after a day spent in a barn, their group was awakened suddenly and given the order to move out at once. The area they were in was particularly dangerous, deep inside enemy territory. The partisan guides were anxious to get them up and going early and quickly so they could cover as much distance as possible before daybreak. After the group, still groggy with fatigue, had walked several kilometers, the parents realized that their older son, then twelve, was not with them. They remembered waking him up; he must have fallen back asleep again. The partisan guides flatly refused to go back for the boy. The parents knew they couldn't take the risk of dropping out of the group and going back on their own. In despair, they could only hope for a miracle. Perhaps another group coming through the village where they had slept would come upon the boy and take him along with them and maybe they would someday find him again.

That is in fact how it worked out, but not before something worse had happened. When the young son who had been left behind awoke and found himself alone and abandoned by his own parents, deep inside enemy territory, far away from home, the shock was too much and something in his mind gave way. The next group coming through the village did indeed pick him up and several months later, after passing through the front line, he was reunited with his family. But the boy had withdrawn into himself. When I first met the family four years later, in a camp for displaced persons in West Germany, the boy, who was by now sixteen, had still not emerged from his withdrawal and rarely spoke to anybody, except himself. He had obviously become a mental case, but the kind, people said, who "wouldn't hurt a fly." Suddenly, one fine day two years later, the boy did emerge, with a vengeance. He turned on his family with a knife and forced them to abandon him once more, this time in a mental institution. Later that same year, the parents and the brother left for Israel.

The group from Katlovtse forest encouraged Motl and me to join them, and, with the permission of the partisans, we did. When, after several days' march, we got close to a village where we might halt and rest, the partisans—or "guides" as everyone in the group called them—would go on ahead to find out which households could and would take in a member or two of our group, until a place to stay had been found for everyone. We would usually stay over for only two or three days before moving on to the next village.

I particularly remember one village in which we stayed. It was fairly large, as villages go, and relatively well-to-do, and situated on an enbankment high above a large lake. The people were friendly, we felt quite welcome, and so we stayed there longer than usual, five or six days.

The people I was put up with were a middle-aged couple who had a ten-year-old son. Sharing their hospitality with me was a Jew from the Russian town of Pleshchenits, a gentle, soft-spoken man about thirty-five years old. He'd lost his wife and children early on to the Nazi killers, who had begun liquidating Soviet Jews in captured areas as early as 1941. The man had somehow managed to escape. He spoke little, his quiet demeanor no doubt largely a consequence of his loss. His eyes seemed to reflect suffering and constant sadness. I too had suffered family losses and so I understood and empathized with him. By trade, the man was a mason and ovenbuilder.

One evening the head of our host peasant family told us the story of how he had been saved by a Jewish family in the eastern part of Poland. He had been taken prisoner by the Germans at the very beginning of the war and, along with other Russian soldiers sharing the same fate, was forced to undertake a long march westward. Day after day they walked, sleeping out in the open and making only brief stopovers at transit camps. Before long they were starved and exhausted, and the man knew he wasn't going to make it if things didn't change. (I was quite familiar with the conditions he described, having been obliged to work at the transit camp in Kurenits back in August and September 1941.)

The man made up his mind he would try and escape, and he managed to do so. He then immediately realized that unless he could somehow get rid of his old army uniform and find less conspicuous garb, the odds were that sooner or later he'd be recaptured. Looking for a change of clothes, he knocked at the door of a Christian house and asked for help and was turned away. Then he knocked at the door of another house and this time was lucky enough to find people—Jewish people—who gave him old but serviceable clothes, fed him, and acted as lookout for him so he could slip out of town unnoticed. Now that he looked like an ordinary peasant, the man was able to start the long walk east. He made it over the two hundred or so kilometers to where he lived and that was how he'd been saved.

Our host concluded his story by saying how indebted he felt to Jews and that was why he was particularly glad to have us as his guests. Of course, this made us feel good, too. We were happy, for him and his family, that he had been saved and proud that Jewish people had played a part in this happy outcome. And then I thought about the Jews I didn't know who had helped the stranger knocking at their door and made it possible for him to have the chance he needed to return to his family. I wondered if any of these good people were still alive. Considering the fate of the Jews in my hometown and in all the towns and cities I knew of, probably not.

Our host family made us feel even more welcome after the mason built them a new oven. I served as his helper and brought water up from the lake to mix the cement and handed the man the bricks as he worked. Our host had bought the bricks before the war and then had stored them away because he could find no skilled person to build his oven for him. Most of the artisan-ovenbuilders from before the war had been Jews and now they were all gone, having retreated with the Russian army or having been liquidated by the Germans. Our host could not believe his good fortune when my friend announced he was an ovenbuilder and would be pleased to build our host's long-postponed oven. It took the ovenbuilder and me only a day to dismantle the old clay oven and construct a brand new brick oven in its place. The ovenbuilder from Pleshchenits was clearly a master of his trade and this oven was his masterpiece, as our host proudly boasted afterwards, when he told people how he now had the finest oven in the village.

We next reached the village on the Dvina that everybody referred to as the "jumping-off place" about midday. There were only six houses left in it; the other twenty or so had been burned down by the Germans during a raid several months earlier. We settled down for the night and then, a few hours later, a contingent of twenty armed partisans, leading a group of about a hundred civilians—all of them members of partisan families—pulled in. They had come from a partisan area about 150 kilometers away and were going to the front line, too. We asked if we could join up with them and they accepted us.

After a good rest, the next day we started out again with them at sundown. The weather had turned warmer and the ice on the Dvina River, though still frozen solid enough for people to walk on, was covered with a thin layer of water. The Dvina is fairly broad here, at least 400 meters from one bank to the other. When we got to the other (eastern) side we were in a kind of no-man's-land. Here we had first to pass through a fairly large village that seemed to have gone through the war unscathed; every house was intact. Somehow they had avoided taking hits from either the partisans or the Germans.

Our objective that night was to cross a railroad line at a point about thirty-five kilometers further on. We marched steadily through woods and villages and took only one fifteen-minute rest break. Around midnight it started to rain. My sheepskin coat soon became sodden and heavy.

By the time we got to the edge of the woods near the railroad we were to cross, it was almost dawn. We had meant to cross under cover of darkness, so we were way behind schedule.

An open space about 500 meters wide separated the woods we were in from the railroad tracks we wanted to cross. The open space was treeless, with only a few bushes scattered here and there. Five partisans went on ahead to reconnoiter. The rest of us followed at a distance. As we got closer to the tracks, the Germans opened up with light-machine-gun fire. We were expecting this and kept on going. The vanguard was within thirty meters of the tracks. Then the Germans sent up a volley of flares that turned fading night into day and left us out in the open and exposed. That wasn't in the plan.

There was a moment's hesitation whether we should keep on going anyway or fall back. A reluctance to fall back was understandable. We were deep inside enemy territory and the first light of dawn had already touched the sky. This was not the place to be during daylight hours. As we hesitated, suddenly all hell broke loose. Artillery and mortar shells exploded all around us. Machine gun bullets hit the ground nearby. Ricocheting bullets whizzed by us. The way forward was blocked by a lethal cross fire of machine guns and artillery. We had no choice but to fall back into the woods the way we had just come. The moment we reached the trees, the shooting stopped just as suddenly as it was started.

We regrouped and assessed our situation. In the fire-fight, the vanguard of five had been cut off from us and we could see they had been able to slip across to the other side of the railroad tracks. Luckily, we had taken no casualties. But we could not pause where we were, to wait and try again the next night, for instance. The woods were too sparse. And the whole region was dotted with villages, some close together, containing German or police garrisons. So we did about the only thing we could do. We began a retreat back to our starting point, on the far side of the Dvina. We'd be lucky, I thought, to keep one step ahead of the enemy. Once they figured out our predicament they'd be hot after us. I shuddered when I remembered it was all of thirty-five kilometers back to the Dvina, and every inch of the way back was going to be through enemy territory in broad daylight. I was hungry and tired, and I was sure the others were, too. My soggy coat felt like a ton on my shoulders.

We started back at a pretty fast clip. It was soon full daylight, and we were all too aware we were in the wrong place at the wrong time, like sitting ducks. We marched in silence. There would be German garrisons less than a kilometer away. At first we kept together in a compact line but with time the line began to stretch out as people weakened and stragglers fell back. By midday our line extended over a couple of kilometers.

By the time we reached the intact village on the right bank of the Dvina the sun had disappeared behind the treeline, its last traces streaking the horizon. We had been marching for almost twenty-four hours with very little rest and hardly any food, and we had covered at least seventy kilometers. The last twenty-four hours had been warm and there had been rain, so the water covering the ice on the Dvina was now about twenty centimeters deep. We waded across in the afterglow of daylight. Once on the partisan side, we made the rounds from house to house looking for a place to stretch out for the night. We were weary to the bone. Finding an unoccupied spot was never easy in this village frequented by a steady stream of visitors, where only six of the original twenty-six houses remained intact. Now this task was made even more difficult by the arrival, only an hour or two before our return, of a fresh, large contingent of partisans and civilians. They too were ready and eager to try their luck with a journey "beyond the front line."

After a long and exhaustive search I finally located a tiny free spot under the kitchen table in some house. Using a piece of wood destined for the oven as my pillow, I fell asleep as soon as I hit the floor.

Those of us still left from the original group of forty had disbanded and let everyone go their own way, which meant into the partisans for some and into a niche in some villages for others. The larger group—the one with whom we had tried to cross the railroad tracks—was going to stay on in the jumping-off village for a couple of days before coming to a decision about whether to try their luck again. I don't know whether they ever did get across.

Much later, I heard that after our ill-fated effort, very few partisan groups got through to the front line using the old route. At long last the Germans had apparently decided to call a halt to the traffic. Then, within two months, the Russians mounted an airlift into the partisan-controlled territory and arms and ammunition started to flow again over this new route. The old way of supplying the partisans, tortuous, dangerous, and time-consuming as it was, became obsolete overnight. But while it existed it was a vital and heroic part of the partisan effort. The old route had also made it possible for many civilians, and that included many Jews, to get out of German-occupied territory and into Russia. A good number of these people would never have survived the war without that escape hatch. Now, in March of 1943, the old route "beyond the front" ceased to exist and became a part of history.

7

After trying without success to get into a number of partisan units, I finally was accepted into the Utkin brigade, still on the condition that I furnish a rifle of my own, but this time with a different twist. I was told how to go about getting the rifle.

It seems that before the Red Army retreated, they burned down a whole warehouse full of rifles and some of the metal parts remained on the site. The wooden stocks were gone, of course, and some of the rifle barrels had curled up in the heat of the fire and were beyond salvaging, but others that had remained straight might be restored. I was given the name of a carpenter in another village who did this kind of restoration work. There was a catch to it, though. The incinerated warehouse was located almost next to a German garrison. Getting to it would be risky.

I borrowed a horse and sleigh and drove to a spot about a kilometer from the site, which was as close as I dared go so conspicuously. Then I proceeded on foot. I recognized the place by the two masonry walls left standing. This matched the description I'd been given. On the ground lay thousands of rifle barrels, more or less covered with snow.

Some looked like they had been shaped into a curve to shoot around a corner. Most were bent grotesquely out of any recognizable shape. It was the straight ones I was after. After burrowing around for a few minutes, I came up with three straight barrels that appeared to have their aiming mechanisms intact and looked acceptable. I then made off with this booty.

The carpenter made a wooden stock for the best of the three salvaged barrels and mounted it properly. We agreed I would pay him with my second pair of pants—I had been wearing two from the time I left the Vileyka ghetto.

Now I had what looked like a real rifle and it almost was. Only a couple of flaws still needed correction. The main one was that the chamber the cartridges should slide into was corroded and did not let the cartridges all the way in. Until this was corrected, my new rifle could not be fired. But I presented myself at brigade headquarters anyway and was formally accepted. They checked out my salvaged and repaired rifle, noted the flaws, and issued me another one that did work, but only a handful of rounds, because ammunition was in such short supply. I now understood that the requirement that I go and retrieve a barrel from the burned down warehouse so close to the Germans was not so much to get another weapon as to determine how daring and resourceful I was. It had been an initiation test of my fitness to become a partisan. I was pleased I had passed.

I was assigned to company three of the Utkin partisan brigade, stationed in the village furthest to the north within the partisan-controlled area, located only six kilometers from the city of Polotsk. I went to the village and reported for duty.

The commanding officer was a young Red Army lieutenant, about twenty-three years old and a former prisoner of war. The unit also had a political officer *(komissar otryada)*, equal in command authority to the military officer. Just like the Red Army, every partisan unit, down to company level, had a political officer in addition to its military officer. The political officer was responsible for the morale and political reliability of the men in his unit, including the military officer, whose orders the political officer was authorized to countermand if he deemed them politically or even militarily unacceptable. In practice this meant that civilians—because that's what most political officers were—were making command decisions for which they had no training and, typically, little or no aptitude, command decisions that the military officers, who did have the right training, were clearly better able to make. This structure of dual leadership obviously lowered the fighting ability and performance of the units.

In the middle of the war—I think it was 1943—the Russians recognized the weakness of the system and took steps to correct it. Parity of command authority was abolished and thereafter the political officer was limited to such tasks as extolling the virtues of Communism, exhorting the men to be brave and heroic in battle, and keeping an eye open for political deviance. Nonetheless, the influence of the political officer—the watchdog of political purity—remained high.

Before the war, the man who was political officer in my new company *(otryad)* had been a minor party official. He was now about forty-five years old, he stood no higher than four foot ten or eleven, and his opinion of himself was as elevated as his stature was diminutive. Behind his back, the men called him "little Napoleon." I had only one run-in with him—the second day I was in the company.

I had been assigned guard duty for the period from eight in the evening until midnight. My special orders were to let no one pass who did not give the password. The other Jewish members of the company had warned me to be careful because newcomers on guard duty were often subjected to spot checks to see how closely they were following their orders.

At about ten o'clock I saw a figure approach my post, which was situated in front of the political officer's house. The figure was small and as it drew closer I thought I recognized the silhouette against the snow as the political officer himself. At the proper distance, I ordered him to halt and give the password. There was no response and he kept on coming towards me.

"Halt, or I'll shoot," I yelled.

"I don't know the password," the man answered testily and kept right on coming.

"He's testing me," I thought. I rammed a round into the chamber of my rifle and for the third time I ordered him to halt. Still he kept on coming. So I fired into the air above his head. That stopped him all right.

"Are you crazy? Don't you recognize your own political officer?" he cried out.

"Advance no closer than three meters from me and halt, so I can get a look at you," I said. He did as he was ordered. "I now recognize you," I said. "You may pass."

I continued to pretend I hadn't recognized who it was earlier. He strode away muttering something like, "Think you can shoot at your political officer, do you! I'll show you!"

When I was relieved of duty, about two hours later, I reported the incident to my squad *(otdelenie)* leader. He smiled and reassured me. "You did the right thing," he said. "I'd have shot the son of a bitch." The other men present expressed similar feelings about the political officer. I was amazed how strongly he was disliked. And, contrary to what I'd feared, the man caused no problems for me, then or later. He may not have liked me, but apparently he respected me.

And so I settled in as an active partisan. After a couple of weeks, I understood that the others accepted me: I was one of them.

Our company consisted of 350 fighters. Most were younger men, eighteen to thirty years old, but there were a few middle-aged men among us. Of the 350 no more than about a dozen had non-combat, or support, duties such as preparing food, being in charge of food supplies, making and repairing boots, and so on. The company was organized into six platoons and each platoon *(zvod)* organized into five or six squads.

The squad I was in drew twenty-four-hour guard duty about once a week. We would move en masse to the guardhouse for our post assignments. Four hours on, four hours off. For duty, we donned specially provided felt boots *(volenki)* and a heavy sheepskin coat *(shuba)*. It was a very cold winter and these helped considerably. Yet the temperature sometimes dropped so low—minus 30 degrees Celsius—that a four-hour tour standing outdoors and immobile—as was required at some of the posts, to maintain cover—left me so frozen that there was barely time in the guardhouse to thaw out before it was time to go back to my post again. There were straw mattresses in the guardhouse for us to sleep on, if we could.

There were many guard posts and in time I got to know them all. One was located in a desolate village about four kilometers to the northwest. The squad would be assigned up there only about once every fortnight. The village had been burned down by the Germans in the summer of 1942 and only one house remained standing. Guard duty here wasn't considered too hard. When we weren't at our posts, we could use the house that still stood to rest up in and catch up on our sleep.

This burned-down village and the road connecting it to our base were considered to be the most likely approach the Germans would take if they ever decided to attack us. The road ran through a thick forest. Over a period of several weeks, the partisans felled maybe as many as a hundred trees and laid them across the road to make it impassable to vehicles. We ourselves had no vehicles to send down the road and our men, who moved on foot or on horseback, had no difficulty getting around and through the felled trees. An enemy force with horse-drawn wagons and motor trucks would be hard put to get through and then only slowly.

The toughest guard assignment was the post located practically at the outskirts of the city of Polotsk, about six or seven kilometers from our base. This was not a permanent post. It was manned only when an enemy attack was considered likely. A group of three partisans would be sent there for a long watch of six or eight hours, after which either they would be relieved by a fresh group or, if the emergency had passed, the post would be abandoned again. I put in duty there only twice during what was left of the winter, at a time when the snow was about two feet deep. We made ourselves a fire to keep warm, and from the edge of the woods we could see some of the houses of the city and keep track of the trains entering and leaving Polotsk.

The days we weren't on guard duty, we received practical military instruction. We learned how to aim a rifle properly and shoot at targets from different distances. We learned the names for each part of our weapons. We learned how to break a rifle down, clean it, and put it back together again, and we practiced until we could do this blindfolded. Then we advanced to machine guns, where emphasis was placed on the heavy, water-cooled weapon called a Maxim gun. There were special classes on gaining proficiency in the use of explosives.

Our armament consisted of no more than a few mortars of various calibers, from light to heavy. Like most of the other partisan brigades we had no artillery. Only a few brigades had managed to capture both light pieces, in the course of an attack on a German garrison, and enough shells to make a difference during a drawn-out battle. Access to a further supply of shells was next to impossible.

Michael Zamkov, a friend of mine who was a partisan

in the area of the city of Novogrudok, told me that his brigade had acquired two tanks, which they pulled out of a lake where the retreating Russians had ditched them to keep them from falling into German hands. After coming out of the water, the tanks were taken down, cleaned, oiled, and reassembled, ready for service. Their fighting capacity was still limited, however, due to lack of ammunition, and this made their usefulness more psychological than material. It was understood that enemy policemen, especially those assigned to the smaller, less fortified garrisons, trembled in their boots whenever they heard these partisan tanks clank and rumble by.

About this time, our company came into possession of a 37-millimeter anti-tank gun, stripped from an abandoned Russian tank. I was excited to hear about this, but disappointed when I laid eyes on the weapon, which had been mounted on an ordinary wagon, like a proud orphan in hand-me-downs. For some reason, the gun had been mounted so that it pointed at the horse that drew the wagon. Consequently the horse would have had to be unhitched and then led out of harm's way if the thing was ever to be fired. Not exactly a mounting with quick use in mind. Moreover, the aiming mechanism had been wrecked; the gun had to be aimed by sighting along the barrel. Not exactly a method that promised accuracy. And as a final indignity, the gun had only five shells to go with it, and that made testing and training impossible. I thought of the sawed-off rifle Motl had had back in Katlovtse forest and wondered whether, in a pinch, this gun would prove any more reliable.

When the actual baptism of fire came two months later—when a large force of Germans, including four tanks, was advancing on our base—this gun proved itself quite the equal of Motl's rifle. It refused to fire a single shot, either because the firing mechanism was inoperative or because the shells had been submerged too long.

The real threat we posed to the Germans lay in our hit-and-run tactics, and for this the light armaments we had were quite adequate. We seldom held any garrison town or village we took for long. What we overran by dark of night, we usually abandoned in the morning. If the enemy decided to take back a lost position and brought in artillery and tanks, we simply faded into the landscape and hit him again the next night, either in the same place or elsewhere. After a few such experiences, the Germans were sometimes persuaded to abandon certain garrisons altogether.

Psychologically, the winter of 1943 was not easy for us. Guard duty in inclement weather was draining, while being cooped up indoors the rest of the time was stressful for young men. After the classes and exercises were completed, there was too much time left and nothing really to do. Monotony and boredom were about to take their toll.

So it was with a feeling of joy and hope that the first signs of spring were greeted, as in the beginning of April the relentless grip of the cold gave way to more moderate temperatures. Patches of meadow broke through the snow as if defiantly showing its displeasure at being covered up all these winter months. Crocuses were flowering in the fields and the song of the robin was heard again. By the end of the month, spring was definitely in the air, and we began to look forward to the enjoyment of the warmer weather ahead. It was a calm spring morning; not a cloud in the pale blue sky. Along the dark tree branches, silver leaf buds were poised, ready to burst open. It was the kind of day that makes you feel happy and bouncy and glad to be alive.

At nine o'clock, a messenger on horseback burst out of the woods and galloped up to the commanding officer's quarters. The Germans were bearing down on the base in force from the burned-down village to the northwest. As expected, they were taking the road across which the partisans had felled trees, a few of them mined, and into which the partisans had dug pits, also mined. This would slow the enemy advance but would not stop it. It was reported that the Germans were using some kind of mechanized saw that allowed them to cut through heavy tree trunks in a matter of minutes. (At this time none of us had ever seen or heard of chain saws.)

Our whole company went on alert at once. We took our assigned places around the perimeter of the base, some in trenches that had been dug over the previous year and recently improved and extended, some in bunkers that had been outfitted with heavy machine guns. The mortars and light machine guns took their places. The people of the village evacuated their houses and fled into the woods. Twenty minutes after the first alert, the village was empty and all our men at the ready. Our forward positions were separated from the forest where the Germans were expected to emerge by an open space about 600 meters wide.

Two hours passed. Scouts now brought in reports from which it was estimated that the enemy force consisted of at least eight hundred men, four tanks, and many trucks—a much larger contingent than the first report had suggested. In the face of this superior force, our commanding officer reevaluated his strategy. It would be impossible to defend the village, so he decided to offer only token resistance and withdraw at the first opportunity. Our goal would be simply to inflict as many casualties as we could.

The commanding officer also sent runners to contact a partisan brigade that was out on training exercises just a few kilometers away to ask them for their assistance. But the runners couldn't find them. The other two companies of our own brigade were pinned down by enemy pressure in their own sectors at this time and couldn't come to help us either.

Two platoons—almost half our company's strength— were withdrawn from the trenches and given new orders. I was one of these men. Our orders were to circle around to the northwest and come out on the road behind the enemy. There we would set up an ambush and lie in wait until the enemy had turned around and was heading back. They would not be on the lookout then and, it was hoped, our chances of inflicting casualties would be greater. It was in theory a classic tactical envelopment.

We moved out on the double, under the command of the other platoon leader. Besides our rifles, we took with us four light machine guns and two anti-tank grenades. The heavy machine guns stayed in the bunkers. We took no mortars because they would be ineffective inside the forest. On our way out, we passed the 37-millimeter anti-tank gun, looking quite spiffy as it sat poised and ready. It was manned by my platoon leader, who had been a lieutenant in the Red Army tank corps before the war. The gun had been positioned on a small rise that gave it better sighting, no doubt, but also left it exposed. As we hurried by I gave the gun a quick pat for good luck.

Before we disappeared into the trees, I turned around and took one last look at the village and the trenches and bunkers where my comrades-in-arms awaited the German attack, now believed to be about a half-hour away. It was as if I was trying to engrave the scene in my memory, perhaps aware somehow, below the level of consciousness, that it would not look like this the next time I saw it.

We were about two kilometers from our base village and still one kilometer away from the road when the first sounds of battle reached us—a few timid rifle shots, as if unsure of their timing, like the percussion section of an orchestra misreading a new conductor's downbeat. Then we heard the sounds of heavier instruments—the ra-ta-ta-ta of our heavy machine guns and the thud of our mortar rounds, intermingled with the sounds of the German tank guns firing and their shells exploding. The exchange became quite heavy for a moment and we paused, as if we could make out what was happening by listening closely to the din.

Then we went on again, hoping and praying our comrades weren't faring too badly.

In another ten minutes we reached the road. The noise of the unseen battle continued unabated for a few minutes more and then began to die away, at first gradually, then completely.

I looked down the road and was amazed to see to what extent it had been cleared of obstacles. Huge sections of the tree trunks had been cut away and shoved to the side of the road. We began to move down the road cautiously, in the directon of our base. Our platoon leader and our squad leaders soon found what they considered a good place for an ambush. My platoon took positions on and around a small rise on the west side of the road, protected by a growth of trees of all sizes and by undergrowth, into which we could break off the fight and disappear if need be—one of the prime requirements of ambush against a superior force. The other platoon continued down the road and took up positions about three to four hundred meters away.

The shooting had now completely stopped, the battle presumably over. The outcome? The few words we exchanged among ourselves expressed our concern.

And then we thought of nothing but the upcoming encounter. Our two machine guns had been positioned to have a clear field of fire and still remain camouflaged. The air was heavy with tension. Time seemed to stand still.

We waited.

Almost an hour went by before we heard the first clunk and clatter of approaching tanks and the steadier rumble of motor trucks. The order came down to recheck our weapons and our camouflage. Then, through the trees, the first tank drove into view. The plan was for the other platoon, up ahead, to let the leading edge of the enemy column get alongside our position. We would open fire and then they would join in at the sound of the first shot. Battles rarely follow the predicted scenario, as I was to discover many times during my stint as a partisan. Here, however, it looked like everything was falling into place just as we had planned.

The German column passed by our first platoon position without noticing anything and kept on coming toward where we were waiting for them. I could plainly see the top half of a German officer standing in the open hatch of the leading tank. He looked straight ahead, apparently quite unaware that dozens of partisan eyes were tracking him. Three motor trucks loaded with German soldiers followed the tank. Behind these, I could make out a second tank with maybe a third tank, disabled, in tow.

Kolya, one of our partisans, had hidden under branches in a depression right by the side of the road. He leaped up and tossed an anti-tank grenade at the lead tank. This was our cue. We opened fire with our rifles and machine guns. The grenade hit the rear of the tank. A tremendous explosion at the tank shook the ground under us. A second explosion ruptured the gas tank and the tank was enveloped in orange flames. Stunned, we paused just a moment in our firing.

Fragmentation grenades were hurled into the trucks. In the back of the first one, I saw several German soldiers crumple over and fall to the ground, where they lay like sacks of potatoes. Other German soldiers clutched at their wounds, their mouths agape, making screams that were drowned out by the din of the battle. Still other German soldiers, apparently unhurt, jumped down out of the trucks, only to be cut down by our rifles and machine guns as they touched the ground.

I kept firing my rifle as quickly as loading and aiming permitted and so did the others. It was almost unbelievable that so much could happen in such a short stretch of time. Barely a minute had passed since the first explosion that started it all.

And then the Germans recovered from the shock and

initial confusion of our attack and began to return our fire in a more confident and organized manner. In fact, their shooting became more concentrated and intense by the second. Then the two tanks that remained also opened fire. Trees were cut in half and limbs and branches came crashing down all around us. The tide of battle had definitely turned; the moment had come to break off the fight. The order was given and we melted away into the forest growth. The shooting slowed down, and then stopped completely.

Our platoon stopped about a kilometer away from the road and regrouped. Everybody was accounted for and we had suffered no casualties. We could hear the sound of enemy trucks and tanks moving away. They had taken a beating. We were ecstatic. By our count, there were at least ten dead Germans and at least as many wounded.

Presently the other platoon joined us. They too reported enemy casualties. Unfortunately they also had lost one of their own men, Sasha. Sasha had rushed at one of the tanks with an anti-tank grenade but was cut down before he could throw it. The grenade, armed, fell from his hand and exploded on contact with the ground. His body was ripped to shreds. There wasn't much left to recover when a couple of partisans returned for the body.

We started back toward our base village. Everyone congratulated Kolya on his flawless performance. He was our hero. He had come away without a scratch. The proximity of the explosion left him somewhat shaken and affected his hearing, but that proved to be only temporary. By the next morning, he was his old self again, with no more than a sore shoulder from all the backslapping he received from us and, later, from all the company, in recognition of his heroic accomplishment.

It was some time before I realized how lucky Kolya had been to come out of the encounter not only alive but unscathed, and I think it took him a while to realize it, too. We learned shortly that another partisan, this one from the other half of the company we had left at the village perimeter, also paid with his life after using his anti-tank grenade. Nonetheless, he had succeeded in disabling the tank. This meant that two of our fellow partisans had been killed the same day attempting to do just what Kolya had done. One of the two had failed in his mission, the other had succeeded, yet both paid with their lives.

Later on, when I was in battle with another brigade, I also lost another comrade-in-arms to the same weapon. We began to call anti-tank grenades "suicide weapons" and used them as little as possible. They are different from the small, fragmentation grenade, which explodes four to six seconds after the pin has been removed. The anti-tank grenade works on a different principle. After the pin is pulled, the grenade is armed and will explode on contact with just about anything, even water. We heard of partisans who had thrown an anti-tank grenade from forest cover and had been blown up when the grenade accidentally touched a leaf or a twig in its flight. Moreover, the thing had an awkward shape and weighed nearly two kilos. Because it was so unwieldy you could not throw it very far, which meant you had to get close to whatever it was you wanted to blow up.

At the moment we were approaching our base village on the way back. We came out of the woods and into the open. A few houses in the distance were on fire. Otherwise, quiet reigned and there was no movement. Our two platoons from the road ambush seemed to be the first to return to the battlefield here, which lay between us and the village. As we got nearer, I recognized the wagon that had carried the 37-millimeter anti-tank gun. It was still in the same spot, but overturned, with two wheels in the air.

We passed the outermost trench and came upon the dead body of one of our partisans. Later we learned he had attacked a German tank with an anti-tank grenade and disabled it when the explosion snapped one of the tank's treads. He was killed by German fire when he tried to get out of the trench.

We passed the overturned wagon that had carried the anti-tank gun. About a hundred meters beyond, we came upon the body of my platoon leader, who had stayed at the base to man the weapon. He died trying in vain to get the gun to fire. He must have been making his escape when he was hit point-black by a tank shell. The explosion had blown away part of his torso and the gaping chest was still smoldering.

In one of the bunkers we discovered the body of our only woman partisan. She had been part of the machine gun team in the bunker and was shot in the head when a bullet found its way through the narrow gun slit.

There was one other fatality—a Jewish man about forty-eight years old, whose family name was Shulman and who came from the town of Molodechno, like my mother. He had joined us a month earlier. I had known him slightly when I was a child and he would occasionally come by our house in Kurenits to visit. His body was discovered by the remainder of the company when they returned sometime later. There were no wounds on the corpse. Given his age and the fact that he was overweight, death most likely came from a stroke or a heart attack.

Our commanding officer returned with the remainder of the company and he looked pleased when he heard the report of our ambush up the road. He and several of his staff went up to check the site in person. They came upon the burned-out tank and found it still too hot to touch. They also came upon pools of blood that confirmed enemy casualties.

Blood was also noted within the village, indicating that the partisan defenders had inflicted further enemy casualties. There was no doubt that this had been an important victory for us. A few days later partisan intelligence reported that the number of enemy dead was twenty-seven, with thirty-two more wounded. Kolya was eventually awarded an important Russian medal and so, posthumously, was the partisan who died disabling the tank from the outermost trench at our base.

And now the day was drawing to a close. Nature seemed to heighten the day's events with a brilliant display of colors. As the last rays of the sun disappeared below the horizon, the sky above it was set ablaze with rich red and ocher, creating a scene of extraordinary beauty. Then came twilight, that gentle pause between day and darkness. A trace of light still lingered in the air, faintly edging the trees and setting fire to the underside of one last cloud. The air shimmered as if the sun were reluctant to go. Then all that was left was a pinkish memory. Darkness rose out of the woodlands and the last glow of day vanished.

In the tranquility of those last few minutes, I tried to sort out my feelings about what had happened this day. It had been a long, hard, and tiring day for all of us, and especially for a novice like me. There had been many firsts for me this day; my first time in battle, and my first time under fire. It was also the first time I saw people killed and the first time I saw the hated enemy shown to be mere mortals like everyone else. Yes, the Germans died like ordinary folk when bullets hit them or fire burned them. With a gun in my hand, I was on an equal footing with them. For me, the master-slave relationship died on the battlefield that April day.

This had also been my first opportunity to begin to even the score with the Germans for the death of my family and of so many others. This day's action constituted the down payment. I would use the rest of my service with the partisans doing my best to discharge the debt in full.

The day after the battle we gave our five fallen comrades a military funeral and buried them in a common grave. Three rifle volleys marked the event and the political officer gave a eulogy he had prepared, reciting the individual deeds of bravery and sacrifice of self in the struggle with the enemy. But when the political officer came to Shulman, the Jewish partisan, he took it upon himself to malign our fallen comrade by declaring that the man had died "of fright," with the undisguised implication that this Jew—no doubt like Jews in general—was a coward.

I was stunned by such an unabashed exhibition of anti-Semitism on this formal, ceremonial occasion. After all, a eulogy is by convention and by definition a time to speak well of the dead and, if anything, to accentuate the positive. Yet here was the political officer taking advantage of a public occasion, when he should have been speaking on behalf of all of us, to gratuitously vent his private spleen. In doing what he did, the political officer demeaned himself as well as troubling the solemn moment. And yet such a happening must be recorded and remembered, with all the rest, as a part of the way things were.

The political officer of my company, an obvious anti-Semite, was the exception rather than the rule. On the whole, the rest of my company did not exhibit any direct feelings of anti-Semitism towards me, other than an occasional subtle dig as to the fighting ability of the Jews. This feeling, no doubt, resulted from a prejudiced interpretation of the fact that so many Jews were being killed by the Nazis without offering substantial resistance. After a reasonable time, however, when I and the few other Jews in our brigade had the chance to prove our worth in battle, we were fully accepted.

Later I took it upon myself to make an informal investigation into what had actually happened when the maligned man died. I spoke with several of the partisans who had been near him at the moment of his death and during the moments just preceding. Without exception they said he had fought in the trenches just like everybody else. There was nothing at all cowardly in his conduct. When the order came to abandon the trenches and run into the woods, witnesses said it was obvious at once that the heavy-set, middle-aged man could not run as fast as the others. Despite his panting exertions, he soon fell behind them in the dash to the woods. And then, suddenly and perhaps without warning, his heart failed him and he collapsed, dead.

A short time later the political officer was transferred to another unit. I understand it had nothing to do with the unpleasantness at the graveside, although it may have been related to the general dislike of the man by our company.

Our sector quieted down and normal life at our base resumed, with its ever-present guard duty and the classes in weaponry and other military subjects.

Then, one warm, sunny afternoon, the brigade commander and a party of officers from brigade headquarters paid us a visit. Visitors as important as these were rare; something unusual was up.

Presently the whole company was assembled and the brigade commander addressed us. Nine volunteers were needed, he said, for a special assignment: three men from each of our three companies. The first six men had already been selected. The remaining three would be selected now. Volunteers, step forward.

About forty people, myself among them, stepped forward. The brigade commander now said that the special assignment would not be easy. Those who would like to withdraw should step back. More than half stepped back. I stayed forward, in line.

The brigade commander now characterized the special assignment as dangerous and asked those who did not feel up to it to take this opportunity to step back, and they did so, leaving only a half-dozen of us still in line. From these, I and two others were picked out.

We nine volunteers were then taken aside and the plan of operation was explained to us. This mission had been ordered all the way from the Soviet Union and it was as ambitious as it was dangerous. Russian pilots sent over the city of Polotsk had noted how strong the city's anti-aircraft defenses were. Too many planes were being damaged and the success rate of bombing missions was becoming dangerously low. Could partisans relieve the pressure?

Our task, then, was to go to a village about six kilometers away, on the outskirts of Polotsk, and penetrate a German garrison located there that housed all German personnel operating the city's anti-aircraft defenses. Intelligence had determined which buildings these Germans slept in. We were to kill or disable as many as possible by tossing grenades in through the windows. This loss of personnel should cripple the anti-aircraft defenses of Polotsk.

A platoon leader was put in charge of the mission. We were joined by one more partisan, who was to be the key to our success. He was a native of the garrison village and had recently been in and out of it several times. He would be our guide.

Before setting out we were given enough time to have a meal and prepare for the operation. Besides our rifles and submachine guns, each of us was issued six grenades.

When dusk fell, we started out under an overcast sky— perfect weather. But we didn't take the main road to the garrison village. Like all the other roads going north, it had been closed with felled trees and antitank pits. Instead, we went east, passing through a village where a partisan unit of platoon size was stationed. Beyond the village, a corridor through the forest led almost all the way to Polotsk. The corridor had been cleared in preparation for a high-voltage power line and it was about as wide as an ordinary two-lane country road. The Germans wouldn't be expecting us to come this way.

The corridor was wet; in places the water lay three or four inches deep. As much as possible, we hopped from one tree stump to another and took advantage of the occasional log left lying on the ground. I still had to step into a puddle here and there, and my boots, which had once been fairly waterproof, finally became waterlogged. In my mind, the difficulty of the terrain we were traversing somehow transferred itself to the difficulty of our mission and I began to have doubts. Were we really going to be able to slip in and out of the garrison village unharmed? Had the wish to prove myself blinded me to the actual danger of what we were doing?

And then we turned off the corridor and entered the forest, where the ground was firm and dry. After a certain distance we came to a clearing and our guide signalled a halt. As we huddled together, the guide whispered that we were now about a kilometer away from the garrison village. We couldn't see it, but it was there, on the other side of two trees he pointed to in the gloomy distance.

We noticed that the weather looked like it might shift. We had started out in overcast. Now the moon was beginning to show its face briefly, ducking in and out of the clouds as if playing hide and seek, or even keeping an eye on what we were up to. But in the west the cloud cover was still heavy and seemed to be getting heavier. Which force would prevail in the struggle between light and darkness? We made the decision to wait until a clear-cut trend emerged. Should the clouds dissipate, leaving the moon the winner, then the mission would have to be aborted.

The plan called for us to follow a narrow ravine into the garrison village. As we waited, the guide pointed out the direction in which it lay. Locating the buildings where the Germans slept should not prove a big problem. We had been well briefed before we started out, and we had with us a sketch map of the village, marked to show which buildings we were to hit.

A long half hour went by. The moon hadn't shown itself for quite a while, as if it had decided not to interfere with our plans after all. And then a light rain began to fall, the kind of drizzle that usually lasts for some time. Given this added benefit, our operation was definitely on. The rain would muffle some of our inadvertent noise. Maybe some of the guards would have taken shelter, making it easier for us to stay undetected, the chances of dogs being alerted also diminished.

We checked our weapons one last time and then moved out single-file behind the guide and began the descent into the ravine. Once inside we crouched over and moved slowly and cautiously. Shortly, I could make out the outline of some houses no more than thirty meters away. We began to crawl on all fours until we reached a building where our guide signaled for us to stay put while he checked out the street.

Except for the splatter of water dripping off the building, everything was quiet. No barking dogs. So far so good.

Our guide reappeared and indicated where we were on our sketch map. Each of us knew his target. From where we were, mine was the fifth house over on the right. To make sure that the explosions would go off at roughly the same moment, we were each to begin a count to one hundred as we set off toward our assigned targets. At the count of one hundred, we would activate our grenades and heave them in through the windows.

Go. I bent over and ran to the other side of the narrow street. Hugging the walls I counted off the houses. One, two, three, four. I made out the outline of the building I was to take care of.

And then I realized I had completely lost my count to a hundred. I picked it up again at forty, which seemed as reasonable a number as any. When I reached my target house, I was counting in the seventies. I took out three grenades and hung two of them on my belt, in front. I pulled the pin on the third, to arm it. At the count of one hundred I heaved it through one of the two front windows.

The noise of the windowpanes' breaking wasn't at all as loud as I had expected. I armed the second grenade and heaved it in through the other front window. And then I did the same with the third on the side of the house. All this took no more than a few seconds. I started back at a run toward the yard we had started from.

The first explosion went off when I was just one house away from my target. It had a strangely muffled sound to it. Explosions two and three followed closely. I heard other explosions, some near, some far, and then some rifle shots. Ours? Theirs? When I reached the yard, one of our men was already there. Two more soon appeared.

The rain had been a godsend. So far, hardly any response from the Germans. We had taken them by surprise.

The four of us withdrew at a run, using the same ravine we had come by. About halfway to the woods, the first of a number of rockets lit up the night sky. We hugged the ground. Then several machine guns opened fire. But there was no whining of bullets hitting the ground around us or passing nearby. The Germans must be firing randomly, an automatic response for the sake of a response.

We kept crawling until we reached the safety of the woods. One by one the rest of the contingent soon trickled in.

We returned to our base the same way we had come. I realized now, for the first time, that I was thoroughly drenched. In the clear corridor for the power line, there was much less jumping from stump to stump to stay clear of the wetness. Why bother when we were already soaked through? But we appreciated how lucky we had been. There was not one casualty among us. No way of telling, yet, how much damage we had inflicted on the Germans. We hoped it was considerable.

A few days later, we found out the results of our raid. Intelligence reported five Germans dead and twelve wounded. We were all praised and given credit for a job well done, but I, for one, was disappointed, thinking of all the effort and exertion we had put into the operation and the danger we had subjected ourselves to. Intelligence later reported that the final effect of our raid on the city of Polotsk's anti-aircraft defenses was almost nil.

Interlude

I remember once standing guard with a White Russian about my own age, a nice enough fellow. I got along with him fairly well. To relieve the tedium of guard duty and make the time pass, we talked about many things, from girls to the weather to the situation at the various war fronts and then, inevitably, back to girls. At one point he asked me to explain to him why the Jews had acted so passively, why they offered no resistance when they were taken away to be slaughtered.

This was a question many different people had asked me in one form or another during the war and were to ask me many times afterwards. Often people who put this question did so hinting at some supposedly unique Jewish trait—an inability to fight or, worse, cowardice. These people were prejudiced. They were trying to fit the Jews into their own preconceived mold. There is very little you can explain to people like that because they don't really want an explanation and wouldn't accept one if it were offered to them.

Other people, though, are genuinely puzzled. The White Russian on guard duty with me was one of these. I wondered how to answer the question to somebody who was unfamiliar with the history of Jews in Europe, or with the actual conditions Jews have lived under, or with the subhuman status that the Germans forced on the Jews.

I began by explaining that in Eastern Europe Jews had lived as a minority population without the same political rights as others. In Eastern Europe, Jews were not even permitted citizenship until the very end of the nineteenth century. They were vulnerable to the whims and vagaries of political authorities in a way many other people were not, and they had to rely on those authorities for their survival. Furthermore, prevailing conditions had accustomed Jews to living as a minority with a long history of oppression and persecution.

I also explained to him how Jews were a scattered minority in the countries they lived in—unlike the Kurds in Iraq and Turkey, or the Basques in Spain and France, or the Welsh in Great Britain who, locally, were majority populations and had long-standing identification with the regions they lived in. Jews, by contrast, had no place, no location they could call their own.

I reminded him of the historical role of the Christian church in promoting hate and mistrust in the general population toward the Jews in their midst. After centuries, the oppression of the Jews that the Christian churches preached and practiced became institutionalized in law and in social custom. By tradition and cultural convention Jews had long been singled out as convenient and officially sanctioned scapegoats.

The sinister and impersonal logic of anti-Semitism— once formulated and thrust into the open—developed a power and momentum of its own and spread like a disease. It proved resistant to the medicines of logic and the vaccines of truth. Throughout history Jews have been killed for many absurd reasons. For instance, Jews were falsely blamed for the black plague in the Middle Ages; they were also outrageously accused of the ritual murder of Christian children.

Jews had been subject to massacres for centuries, the scope and intensity of which had steadily increased from the time of the medieval Crusades, when the infidel Jews were found to be easier and safer prey than the infidel Muslims. Jewish communities lived with the scourge of pogroms well into the twentieth century.

The National Socialists, who came to power in Germany in 1933, exploited this historical state of affairs and enlarged upon it. They launched a massive propaganda offensive against the Jews, and by the time the war broke out, it was not hard for them to get the acquiescence and even the cooperation of many local populations. People who over the centuries could be incited by one or two rabble-rousers to make a pogrom were likely to be swayed by the mighty German propaganda machine. Jews were stripped of the few legal rights remaining to them. They were confined in ghettos so they would slowly die of starvation and disease.

Even the few Jewish communities that fared somewhat better in the beginning were isolated and unable to communicate with each other. Rumors replaced reliable news. The Germans manipulated information by spreading false rumors and by officially proclaiming the false to be the true. In desperate times people believe what they must to stay sane. It was suggested that maximum cooperation on the part of the Jews would ensure the best chance of survival. It was unbelievable that the Germans were in fact totally committed to the destruction of the Jews.

Did the Jews then go to their death ignorant of what was happening to them? Only at first, perhaps, in the early months of the German occupation, when all the Jewish men and boys of a town would be marched away and simply disappear. The Germans then circulated rumors that the men had been sent to work camps. In fact, the Jewish men had been executed the moment they were out of sight and hearing of the townspeople. When evidence of these mass executions came to light, surviving Jews tended to believe—wanted to believe—it had been a mistake, a fluke.

That thousands upon thousands were being systematically slaughtered went beyond the human capacity to assimilate and comprehend. Even centuries of living with persecution had not prepared us for this horror. Our experience of the last millenium and a half taught us that all persecutions, however cruel, eventually came to an end. The demands of oppressors were ultimately limited and could be met. Never before in their history had Jews faced an enemy that demanded not just some or most of their possessions, but everything; not just a few lives, or even many, but all, down to the last infant. Nothing could prepare people to believe in the existence of something so monstrous.

And yet as word of more and more German "actions" reached us, we knew—we could not help knowing—that something extraordinary and horrible was taking place. But there is a vast difference between being intellectually aware of something so terrible and of believing it. Maybe there is a kind of insulation or anesthetic built into us to make it possible to live with the unthinkable and the unbearable: psychological denial of what we nonetheless knew must be the case. Maybe it's the same for a group as it is for the individual who, in heightened reaction to danger, does not feel physical trauma at the time it occurs and only later experiences pain.

You hear someone tell how all the Jews in a certain town have been massacred and how this person who is telling of it has been the only one in their family to escape. You hear this and you know it must be true, but you do not allow the implications to sink in, because if you did, your cognitive world would collapse and you would fall apart. You would be unable to cope at all. At the very least, facing up to things as terrible as these puts hope in intolerable jeopardy. It is denial and hope—a belief in the impossible if need be—that keeps people going under such extreme stress. Without hope, without irrational hope if necessary, some people would lapse into the living death of immobilized depression.

And so, little by little, the truth that was at first denied refuses to be ignored any longer. More and more stories circulate of what the Germans are doing to the Jews, and it becomes less easy to dismiss them all. But as long as the protective mechanism built in by nature still operates, people cling desperately to hope, however feeble. Even when the chances for survival are getting more remote with every passing day, you still hope that somehow *you* will miraculously survive. Most people seem to have a built-in belief in personal exemption. "Maybe if I work hard enough and diligently enough, they'll let me live." "Maybe the war will end soon, and I'll be saved." "Maybe the new Russian offensive will send the Germans retreating so fast they won't have time or inclination to bother with us remaining Jews, and I'll be saved." Maybe, maybe, maybe. Always the nourished spark of hope.

Organized resistance to the Germans, such as building barricades and in an organized manner actively resisting an "action," was not possible, but individual resistance, usually born of sudden desperation, was not rare. Individual persons might try to attack and kill the one or two Germans, or policemen, sent to arrest them. A few might succeed and then escape to the forest, but the brutal reprisals visited on their family and relatives, or their town, discouraged others from following their example.

There is nothing inherently Jewish about the way these millions of people responded. Had the same calamity befallen any other people in similar conditions, the outcome would have been the same. In fact, something similar did happen to another group of people, and the results were the same. It was well known that the German armies took vast numbers of Russians as prisoners of war, and that most of these Russians offered no resistance whatever and subsequently perished. The full scope of the calamity did not become known until after the war, when it was established that six to eight million Russian soldiers had been captured and that three-quarters of them had been killed by starvation, disease, or execution, in Auschwitz and other extermination camps.

But many of these Russian prisoners, I reminded the White Russian on guard duty with me, were trained and battle-tried military men, and most of them were vigorous young men in the prime of life. They had the further advantage of not being responsible for one another and for having no family obligations since their families were not with them. They were also of the same background as the general population. Surely, it would seem that these Russian prisoners of war could have revolted. And yet they did not. It was for them as it was for the Jews. The conditions the Germans imposed were so harsh and all-encompassing that resistance by either group was not possible.

I thought I detected a spark of comprehension in the eyes of my fellow guard. After a long moment of silence, he said he thought he had a better understanding about the seeming passivity and non-action of people so disoriented and dehumanized.

After the war and the Nuremberg trials, much new information became available. Many Nazi documents surfaced that shed light on Hitler's plans for the "final solution of the Jewish problem"—the annihilation of the Jews—Hitler's prime objective, as he announced to the world time and again in his speeches and writings, even before the war. In documents signed by Himmler and Heidrich, the orders for genocide were invariably expressed in euphemisms or in code, such as, "final solution of the Jewish problem," "evacuation [of the Jews] to the east," *"Judenaktion,"* "special treatment," "resettlement," and so on.

The atrocities committed by the Nazis against the Jews, the gypsies, the Russian prisoners of war, and millions of others were on such a vast scale and so mind-boggling in their thoroughness as to be virtually unbelievable. The discovery of death camps and mass execution sites—Auschwitz, Treblinka, Maidanek, Babi Yar, the Ponary hills near Vilno, and countless others—shocked the world. Each of the German factories of death was organized with typical German efficiency and used the most up-to-date technology. The death factories processed tens of thousands of live human beings daily and turned them into smoke and ashes.

Even those of us who had been lucky enough to survive and who had gone through hell on earth trying to escape the death planned for us time and again by Hitler's killers were all shocked. Our individual experiences should have prepared and conditioned us for any new revelations about the Jewish tragedy. Nonetheless, we were still shocked and astounded by the enormity and bestiality of the crimes (which we all experienced personally to some degree): by the meticulous planning that went into the killings, by the great amount of resources allocated, by the high priority assigned to the execution of the death plans, and by the death factories, where death—the principal product—was produced daily in such high volume, by the psychological onslaught on the victims, so well planned and carried out so systematically. All this contributed to the Nazi "success" in this area and helped to lull their victims into inaction. The machinery of lies and deceit that the Germans instilled to make the Jews feel—until it was too late—that hope for survival was to be found in being docile and peaceful played a large role in the general scheme of events. The Germans were so successful in this charade that the victims often did not realize until the last moments of their lives that they were being led to slaughter.

One of the better-known German slogans deliberately

created to mislead and confuse was *"Arbeit macht frei (Work is liberating),"* posted on the entrance gates to their extermination camps to suggest that one was merely coming into a work camp. Other signs posted on the way to the gas chambers instructed people to lay their clothes down in an orderly fashion to avoid problems in finding them again "after the shower." But, as the victims discovered presently, the "shower heads" emitted lethal gas.

There seems to have been no limit to the obsessive ingenuity and imagination that the Germans devoted to inventing ways of spreading disinformation and confusion—all to keep the victims ignorant of their fate as long as possible, to pacify them so that flight or rebellion would never come to mind. Jews from recently "resettled" towns and ghettos were persuaded or forced to write letters back home telling of the fine treatment they were receiving in the new places, after which the letter writers were soon shot, gassed, burned alive, or killed in any of the many other ways the German mind had discovered and perfected.

The Germans were, after all, a highly organized nation, capable of waging war almost single-handedly against the entire world, and they were bent on annihilating the Jewish minorities in all the lands under their rule. That a small remnant of European Jewry managed to survive against such overwhelming odds is nothing short of miraculous. It is also nothing short of miraculous that under such impossible conditions Jews were still able to organize uprisings, in the ghettos and even in the death camps, all with little or no hope of success other than in the spirit of the biblical Samson "to die with the Philistines."

The best known of these uprisings took place in the Warsaw ghetto, where the Jewish fighters held out for several weeks against Waffen-SS troops armed with artillery, tanks, and planes. The Jewish fighters killed scores of German troops and destroyed many tanks and troop carriers. Uprisings also took place in the death camps of Treblinka and Sobibor, and in other, lesser known death camps and ghettos.

When Jews managed to break out, as they did in a few instances, often elements of the local population would promptly notify the Germans or the police, or would themselves grab the fleeing Jews and hand them over to the authorities. In reality, the Jews were kept in the camps and ghettos by the hostility of the local populations as much as by the Germans. The few Jews who reached what they thought was the safety of the woods, were then, often as not, set upon by the notorious *Armia krajowa* (AK) that gave allegiance to the Polish government-in-exile in London. The AK ranged throughout the forests of Poland and, to some extent, the forests of White Russia, up to the old Polish-Russian border. They made war on the Jews with more zest than they made war on the Germans, and they were responsible for the deaths of hundreds and possibly thousands of Jews, who, upon finally reaching the woods and innocently asking to join the ranks of what they thought were friendly partisans, were instead gunned down.

8

On May 4, 1943 orders came down for a detail of nine to be selected from our brigade—three persons from each of our three companies—and for this detail to be sent on guard duty for a month to a food depot we hadn't even known existed until that moment. I was among those selected. It was then explained to us that this cache of food had existed for almost a year and was the result of a cooperative effort by several partisan brigades, which took rotating monthly turns guarding it. The food was meant for emergency use, in case the partisans were cut off from existing supply lines. It was located deep within a forest, in Ushachi county.

A squad leader was assigned to our group and we walked twenty kilometers to a forest village near the food depot, but far from major highways or even country roads. The depot itself was located about three kilometers outside the village. Our group of nine was broken down into units of three and each three-man unit had twenty-four-hour guard duty every third day. For the two full days between tours of guard duty we were on our own.

We were billeted one man to a family among the villagers. We ate with our hosts and were treated like one of the family. Compared with the food we ate at the base, the food here was good. The atmosphere made a relaxing change from the hustle and bustle of base camp, where there was always a certain amount of tension in the air as scouting parties and raiding parties continually came and went. Village existence here was so peaceful in contrast, it was hard to remember there was a war going on.

The villagers, all peasants, worked their fields without interference from anybody. As far as I knew, the Germans never visited this hidden village nor did partisans, except for the guard detachments. I suppose we added a little variety to village life; we were certainly made to feel welcome. In the evenings we would often get together with some of the local girls for a couple of hours of singing, telling stories and jokes, and for a bit of romancing, all of which made for a pleasant change from conditions at our Spartan base camp. I especially remember the Sunday dinners and all the special delicacies that were prepared for us.

Because we had no feeling of danger, even guard duty was no real chore. Each morning the squad leader would accompany a group of three of us to the depot and then return with the group of three coming off duty. The days were pleasantly warm and the nights cool, perfect for sleeping out under the stars at the depot, since I still had my good old sheepskin coat with me. No garment I ever owned served me better. It kept me warm in the winter, both as a coat during the day and a blanket at night. When spring came—and even later during the summer—I carried it around, draped over my arm, wherever I went. With a bed of pine boughs and my sheepskin coat for cover, I knew I could enjoy a good night's sleep just about anywhere.

In its own way, even the twenty-four-hour tour of guard duty was pleasurable. The forest was so peaceful. All you heard were its natural inhabitants, the birds and the squirrels. Besides several varieties of pine, this forest included birch, aspen, and white ash trees. The deciduous trees had budded only a few days before we arrived and the leaves were still tiny. I watched with fascination as the growth progressed. The change was quite noticeable from one tour of duty to the next.

In the evening the forest quieted down even more, assuming a serene and almost dignified manner. At night you could hear the light wind rustling softly in the trees and, from time to time, an owl hooting and the mournful song of another bird, as if decrying the passage of another day. At night we often heard the drone of airplanes and we could tell by the sound whether they were Russian or German. Many times, in the starlight, with or without a moon, I looked up at a patch of sky left open by the tree tops and saw a Russian plane fly over with a string of gliders in tow. If you strained your eyes you could even make out the tow lines connecting them. We understood that these gliders were bringing weapons and ammunition to some partisan unit or other, located, as we were, behind the German lines.

The depot itself consisted of about twenty underground storage bins (*zemlyanki*), each about fifteen to twenty meters long, and up to five meters wide. These structures had been built below ground level. The exposed roofs, which sloped slightly, were camouflaged with sod, vegetation, and forest debris to look from above like the forest floor around it. The storage bins were built out of small and medium sized logs, banked with earth on three sides but visible on the fourth, exposed side where the door was. Inside these bins the partisans had stashed away tons of various grains and cereals—wheat, rye, and barley—plus beans, potatoes, salted meat, and pork fat.

In the village there was an abundance of lilac bushes and they came into full bloom. Their fragrance permeated the air. I am sure that my love of the outdoors, which has remained with me to this day, especially in springtime, when the lilacs are in bloom, was born during that May of 1943, off in that hidden forest village, while we were guarding the food depot. I loved it there and toward the end of the month I began to feel a twinge of sadness that the time we would have to leave was approaching.

Then one day—it was the first or second of June—we could hear the muffled sounds of distant artillery fire. The sounds of war had managed to reach the little village. I was on guard duty and had no idea what it meant, besides realizing that a battle was taking place somewhere. Judging by the sound, it must have been eight to ten kilometers away.

The group of three men that came from the village to relieve us the next morning didn't know much more than we did, except that the Dubrovtsi brigade was supposed to be engaged in battle with the Germans. By our standards the Dubrovtsi brigade was large and powerful. They had four thousand fighters and a large battery of artillery plus a good supply of shells to go with it. It was never clear to me how they had come by the artillery and so much ammunition. They were the only brigade to be in this fortunate situation, so it was almost surely Dubrovtsi artillery we heard. And then the frequency of artillery firing began to diminish even though the sounds became somewhat louder. It was several days before we learned more about what was happening.

A message from our own headquarters soon explained the situation. The Dubrovtsi brigade had been fighting off an enemy assault for close to a week. The Germans hadn't been successful in routing them, but the brigade had had to give up some ground, with the result that the Germans were now positioned no more than five kilometers from the food depot. A full breakthrough was possible. It had been decided that the food supplies would be evacuated. Some three hundred horse-and-wagon teams, mobilized from villages all over the surrounding countryside, would be arriving the next day to begin the evacuation. Construction had already started on a new depot and was proceeding at a feverish pace.

The villagers, sensing that a battle in or near their village might well be in the offing, decided to move to a location deep within the forest. Our squad moved with them and we continued to spend our off-duty hours among them. The village now stood empty. As expected, our tour of duty was automatically extended when no new group came to relieve us at the end of the month.

Meanwhile, the evacuation of the food depot proceeded. It took about a week before the place was fully emptied. During that time the Germans came to within three kilometers, but that was as close as they got during this campaign. Then, slowly but surely, the Dubrovtsi pushed the Germans back. Eventually the Dubrovtsi regained all the territory they had originally held.

While we were away on guard duty at the forest food depot, our company had moved several kilometers away from its base village to serve as support for another brigade that was fending off the enemy. We reported back to our company at this new location and I joined my squad and platoon in the trenches. They had been repulsing enemy attacks for three days, but with our arrival the sector quieted down and one day later our whole company returned to base.

A few days later I happened to visit the home base of the second company of our brigade. They were located in a village seven or eight kilometers away from our own base village, and while I was there, I heard an account of remarkable heroism. About a week earlier, while my group of nine was still on guard duty in the forest, the rest of the brigade had been entrenched at the front line, helping to defend the perimeter. A small hill was being defended by a squad of partisans armed with one heavy machine gun and ten to twelve rifles. They were spotted by the enemy, subjected to artillery bombardment, and then rushed by a platoon-sized group of enemy soldiers, whereupon they abandoned the hill and their machine gun.

Another squad of partisans, located on a hill nearby, saw what was happening. In this squad there was a young Jewish man from the town of Dolhinov, no more than twenty years old. I had run into him a couple of times and knew him slightly. At the mention of the young man's name, the entire group of ten to twelve partisans listening to the story nodded their approval and admiration for him.

When this young man saw that the squad on the nearby hill had abandoned their heavy machine gun, on his own initiative, he ran over and up the hill and took over the weapon, which he then proceeded to fire all on his own—an accomplishment in itself—raking the approaching enemy infantry over an arc of 180 degrees, as he swiveled the gun back and forth. The enemy had seen the squad abandon its position and flee, so this fire took them by surprise. They broke and fled. When the original squad saw what the young man was doing, they took heart and returned to help him pick off a few more of the fleeing Germans. I regret I no longer recall this young Jewish hero's name. I know only that he did not survive the war but fell in battle some months later.

In time I covered much of the Ushachi region on foot and came to be quite familiar with most of the villages. From our base village I could tell in what direction they lay and how far off. So when the evening sky turned red off on the horizon, which meant a fire somwhere, I found I could correctly identify the village where the fire was and specify its distance from us.

In the course of my travels I discovered scattered all over the region a number of Jews, mostly elderly, living one or two to a village and apparently settled in semi-permanently. All were originally from a radius of fifty or sixty kilometers of my hometown of Kurenits and a few of them were from Kurenits itself. Thus, in one village I came upon the sisters Reykhe and Relke Alperovits, whose brother Aaron (Naftolye's) was with the partisans. In another village I found my old bookkeeping teacher, a man from the town of Ilya. He was keeping a journal, then an inch thick, in his beautiful Yiddish handwriting. I was allowed to read a page or two and realized there was material for a very good book here. Alas, neither the man nor his journal survived.

Ruve-Zyshke Alperovits and his wife, from Myadler Street in my hometown of Kurenits, lived in another village. They were the parents of two sons, Eli and Motye. Eli, the older son, had been killed near Kurenits only weeks after he joined the partisans in the summer of 1942. Motye, the younger son and a year my junior, was also with the partisans and I ran into him in yet another Ushachi county village. He told me where his parents were, but the village they were in was too far out of the way for me then and I never got to see them. Motye himself was killed in action toward the end of the summer of 1943. I was shocked and saddened when I learned of it. Eli and Motye had been friends and schoolmates of mine. Both of these brave young men met their death while fighting against our mortal enemy.

Their parents, now childless and broken in spirit and body, survived until the Germans overran the Ushachi region in May 1944. They were then killed, along with most of the seventy elderly or middle-aged Jews scattered over the region. Only four or five managed to survive. The rest were identified as Jews and, as such, executed. Many had been working for the partisans in non-combatant roles, like bakers or teamsters driving supply wagons. Another man I knew operated a tannery and supplied the partisans with leather he made from horse and cowhides. But when the end came, they were all left to fend for themselves, and being in no position to do so, they perished.

An elite company was being organized. Unlike the three other companies in our Utkin brigade, identified only by number, this company was to have a name—the Komsomolski company. It would consist of a hundred or so fighters drawn both from our brigade and from others, organized on the standard triad principle. We were to concentrate on demolition missions, like blowing up bridges, trains, and railroad tracks. All members of the new unit were expected to be young and to excel in demolition work. I qualified on both counts and so was picked out and transferred into it. There were never more than a hundred of us in the company. We were divided into three platoons plus a squad on horseback. Each platoon was in turn divided into three regular squads, so there were only about eight or nine people in a squad most of the time. Compared with other partisan groups, these nominal squads of ours were not particularly close-knit. This was because we operated mostly on special assignments for which ad hoc units of squad or platoon size were put together, according to the individual skills or experience needed for a particular task. Consequently we were frequently working with different people on different missions. In most combat units, including the Germans, the integrity of the squad and platoon is considered crucial.

Our commanding officer had been a party official before the war. He was around forty-five years of age, a soft-spoken man, now developing middle-aged spread—a college professor type, with a fatherly disposition. The men, who never felt he was unreasonable in his demands, liked and respected him. Our company executive officer (in Russian, *nachalnik shtaba*) had been a company platoon leader in the old Utkin brigade. He stood about six feet tall and made an impressive appearance. Like our commanding officer, he too was quiet, intelligent, and respected. I had served under him when he led the successful ambush from our home base in the spring of 1943.

I was becoming quite adept with explosives and it was usually my task, on a mission, to select the kinds of explosives or mines to be used, and to assemble and prepare them. This was a demanding job. Nobody wanted to end up with a dud after all the dangers and difficulties it took to get an explosive in place undetected. And the most extreme care was required at every stage of preparation, from assembling through the final placing.

The explosive we used most often was called, in Russian, *tol*. It looked somewhat like soap, but was harder in consistency. It was lemon-yellow in color and came shaped like a tennis ball, only smaller, with a hole in which to insert a small, pencil-like detonator. Without the detonator the substance was quite harmless. A length of special detonator cord was plugged into the detonator hole, and once lit this cord would burn even under water. *Tol* explosives were used on bridges, small factories, captured food or matériel that would be awkward to burn or cart away, enemy bunkers, and other strongholds.

When the partisans first began blowing up railroads, *tol* was used almost exclusively, and with much success. Many locomotives and cars were derailed, many Germans killed, and great quantities of war matériel destroyed. The mines we used were quite primitive. They consisted of several kilos of *tol* and were triggered by hand, either by pulling on a rope or closing an electric circuit powered by a battery. Either way, one man had to remain nearby to trigger the explosion.

We learned the hard way, from experience, that laying mines and blowing up trains is easier said than done. Just approaching the railroad was hazardous. Laying the mines took a lot of time and concentration, both of which were in limited supply. But to rush a job could lead to one of two undesirable outcomes: the mine would not go off when triggered or, worse, it would go off while being put in place and kill the man or men working on it. But meticulous and careful work, plus a large dose of luck, made success a reasonable possibility.

When we began a mission, we tried to learn as much as we could about the habits of German guards and patrols in the area. Peasant contacts were useful for this. They could move around more openly and freely than we could and get the information we wanted. When a location was finally decided on for an operation, a peasant would often serve as a guide to lead us in. All this took time.

The first operation I was on took a group of seven or eight of us nearly two weeks to bring off, much longer than we had anticipated. Our group leader was a man by the name of Kulik. I got along with him very well and went with him on many subsequent operations. He was respected by both the men and our commanding officer and he had a knack for seeing who would be the right local people to pick as scouts and guides. Still, at the beginning, when we lacked experience, we made a lot of blunders. On this first operation, for instance, we approached the railroad line that was to be our target without either reconnoitering ahead of time or bringing along a local guide. We stumbled on German patrols twice. The second time a shooting exchange followed and we had to pull back, luckily without casualties. Our third try also proved unsuccessful.

On our fourth try we succeeded in planting a mine between two ties under the rail at a spot where the tracks made a long curve. There were five of us. Three stood lookout while the fourth man and I did the actual work. When the mine was in place, we covered it with sand, for camouflage, and let out a length of the rope connected to it. Then we ran down the steep embankment towards the woods, about fifty meters away, letting out rope as we went.

I settled down among the trees to wait and the others took up positions in a wide arc around me to keep a watch for enemy patrols. An hour passed. Then I could hear a train approaching. I tensed and my eyes strained for some movement in the darkness where the sound was coming from. It was becoming louder by the second. Finally I could make out the shape of a locomotive. I was all set to jerk the rope, but at the very last second I held back; there was no train behind the locomotive, so I let it pass.

Kulik came up in the darkness alongside and asked what I thought I was doing, letting the locomotive go by like that. I explained my reasoning to him. It did not pay to waste a well-positioned mine on a solitary locomotive when a regular train might soon follow—for which the solitary locomotive was conceivably a scout or even a decoy. He agreed with my logic but felt we might be pushing our luck too far and I had to agree with him.

Another twenty minutes passed and I could hear another train coming from the same direction as the solitary locomotive that had preceded it. I promised Kulik that I would trigger the explosive no matter what kind of train this turned out to be. Shortly, a silhouette was visible in the darkness. And then I saw that this was a very long train and traveling very fast, and it was getting close to where our mine lay in wait for it. At the last minute I made out that the train was being pulled by not one but two locomotives. Obviously they were hauling something heavy and important. I remember thinking quite clearly there was no way I was going to let myself miss the timing on this one.

I gave a jerk on the rope just as the front wheels of the first locomotive ran over the mine. Close to ten kilos of *tol* went off in an ear-shattering explosion. The front end of the locomotive danced up into the air and then returned to earth on the slope of the embankment beside the tracks. The second locomotive and the cars behind followed the first locomotive down the embankment. Sparks were flying everywhere. Metal grated and screeched on metal. Steam hissed. Somebody was pounding me on the shoulder to urge me to get the hell out of there, but I stood riveted to the ground, fascinated and transfixed by the spectacle, triumphant and proud.

Then there was a second explosion and a fireball began to expand right in front of me while debris spewed up into the orange air along with what looked like huge metal drums. I smelled gasoline and realized I had been smelling it for a while without taking notice. A wave of heat swept over me and I jumped back, still unable to take my eyes off the powerful inferno I had brought into being. I forced myself to break the spell and run off after my comrades. As I ran I could still hear, in the distance, the sound of cars being dragged off the rails before they plunged down to the bottom of the now fiery embankment.

We had done two things right. We had placed the mine at a spot where the track curved and we had placed it on a piece of track above a steep embankment. Both these factors made a large-scale derailment more certain the moment an explosion caused anything to leave the tracks.

We slept the remaining hours of the night and into the morning at the house of one of our contacts, while he went to find out what he could about the derailment. Before the end of the day we had reports from a number of sources, including three separate local contacts plus partisan scouts from a nearby brigade. They all agreed that two locomotives and eighteen to twenty cars had left the tracks and had been made irretrievably useless by the ensuing conflagration. Charred remains showed that several cars had been carrying leather boots and blankets. Two flatbed cars carrying heavy cannon had been turned into junk that could be made out in the general pile-up. Most of the gasoline drums had gone up in flames, but a few had escaped harm and lay scattered over the ground nearby. There was no definite word on the rest of the freight the train was hauling, and no definite word on German personnel losses, beyond the crews of both locomotives. But losses even among a skeleton guard would have been considerable. Traffic on the railroad line was halted for at least twenty-four hours while the salvage crews cleared away the debris and restored the damaged track.

It was another two days before we got back to our village, where a heroes' welcome awaited us; news of our success had preceded us by a full day.

As time went by, the Germans, faced with mounting losses of men, war matériel, and railroad stock, stepped up their vigilance and manpower considerably. Since the last part of a train often survived a derailment, the Germans took to attaching a car full of soldiers to the end of an important train. If anything happened, the soldiers would quickly jump out and scour the immediate vicinity of an accident for partisans and take off in hot pursuit of any found lingering there.

Our methods and equipment were growing more sophisticated, too. We were beginning to receive some fully assembled mines. We were also getting remote detonators and timing devices. Certain detonators could be triggered in response to pressure or vibration on the tracks, thus allowing partisans to be kilometers away when the explosion took place.

The Germans were determined to keep open this most important lifeline to their armies on the eastern front, and so were obliged to take still further countermeasures. By 1944 no trains passed through partisan-controlled land after sundown. During the day, when visibility was reestablished, foot patrols often preceded a train down the track and checked for signs that would indicate mines had been laid during the night. German dogs were trained to sniff out concealed explosives. An empty flatbed car might be attached to the front end of a train and pushed ahead to take the brunt of any explosion and leave the rest of the train more or less intact. Eventually these countermeasures the Germans took succeeded in putting us out of the demolition business, at least in areas near Ushachi county—but at a cost. Thousands of German troops were tied up working as railroad guards and patrols. Rail shipments to the front were slowed down enormously. Thus, the partisan effort was taking its toll even when the primary business of demolition was no longer possible.

We then moved our operations still further to the west, into an area that had belonged to Poland in 1939, before the war. There were many fewer partisans here and so confrontations between Germans and partisans were rarer. Railroads were attacked less regularly and the Germans continued to be casual in their vigilance. Through the remainder of 1943 we operated with a certain degree of success, chalking up twelve derailed trains carrying large quantities of war matériel that were destroyed, including some heavy guns and a whole trainload of new tanks.

My Komsomolski company was sometimes called upon to take part in the more conventional operations that our Utkin brigade conducted. One of these operations, which took place in mid-summer of 1943, was an attack to be made on a large police garrison located in a small town. About 1,500 partisans—the equivalent of two brigades—were to take part. From my company, only my platoon was assigned to the operation, the rest of the company being on extended operations to the West, and we were to be led by the company executive officer. My platoon was ordered to go to a village a few kilometers from the intended target and to remain there until further orders. Three days passed. The strategy behind this delay, if indeed there was one, wasn't clear to me. The police would surely have learned of our presence shortly after we arrived in the village. Maybe the idea was to intimidate the police and get them to leave on their own. If that was it, it did not succeed. The police did not abandon their garrison, and instead, most likely strengthened it.

On the third night, we got orders to advance on the police garrison. It was going to be done the hard way after all. We moved out around ten o'clock, which is when darkness begins to fall in mid-summer at that northern latitude. In summer, true nights are short, lasting no more than three or four hours. The attack on the garrison began in darkness about an hour later, with partisans advancing on it from all sides at the same time and yelling and screaming ''hurrah'' at the top of our voices. This vocal contribution to the attack was customary in the Red Army both before and during World War II. The blood-curdling yell was supposed to strike terror in the hearts of those being attacked and thus weaken their resolve to stand their ground and fight. I'm sure this interesting practice had its uses and may even, at times, have had some of its expected psychological effect. However, in my own experience—and we carried out the practice many times—it was not clear that any positive contribution to an attack ever resulted. I remember thinking that a surprise attack, after advancing on an enemy position as quietly as possible, might have more going for it. But orders were orders and must be obeyed.

We yelled ''hurrah'' at the top of our lungs over and over until we reached the outskirts of the little town in which the police garrison was located. My group took a position behind the wall of a house and we huddled there contemplating our next move. My buddy Vasil and I stayed close together. We had an understanding that we would look out for each other in case one of us got wounded. Within view of where we huddled stood a long, one-story brick building that looked something like a barracks, but was in fact the local school building. Suddenly we were fired upon from the building and two comrades were hit. The rest of us, protected by the house, were out of the line of fire. One of the men hit died on the spot; the other died two days later back at base.

The order came to storm the brick building. First, grenades were tossed in through the windows and then we entered and began clearing the building, room by room. Within fifteen minutes we were through. Of the sixteen policemen we found there, twelve had been killed and the four survivors gave themselves up. Their hands were tied behind their backs and they were marched out to the rear, escorted by one partisan.

As we left the building, we could hear rifle and machine gun fire from the center of town where fighting was obviously still going on. We could see that several rooms of the school building were on fire, most likely because of our grenades. Stored ammunition was beginning to explode in the heat. It was suggested that we could get hit by exploding rifle rounds coming at us through the windows, even though I thought to myself that the chances of that actually happening were pretty remote.

A kind of rough log fence or wall ran along the length of the school building, about three meters away from it. It had probably been built as protection from partisan attack. Now we partisans used it for protection from the explosions inside the school building as we advanced along the exposed side of the fence in a crouched position, led by our executive officer. Across the open field we could make out the dim outline of a bunker, maybe 100 meters away. We would attack it from the rear, after getting to the end of the log fence. I was in the middle of our advancing line. Every so often I glanced over at the bunker. We knew it was manned and it projected a menacing feeling. I remember thinking, "Why aren't we moving along the inside of the fence, instead of out here on the outside, exposed?" The danger of being hit by a stray exploding bullet from inside the burning school building seemed infinitely smaller than being exposed to the machine guns in the bunker.

And then suddenly the bunker let go a short burst of machine gun fire. Those of us in the middle of the line were not overly alarmed, but the men in front started moving backwards with great urgency. In short order we retreated to our starting point behind the house. What had happened? Those around me didn't seem to know. Then we became aware that our executive officer wasn't there. His name was called out several times. No answer. He must be up along the fence. Wounded? Dead?

The platoon leader asked for volunteers to go in and bring the man out. No one stepped forward. He then ordered two individuals—one of them a squad leader—to undertake the rescue. Both refused the direct order, saying that the fence was a death trap.

Disobeying a direct order was a court-martial offense, and especially serious in the midst of battle. Sometimes partisans were shot for such insubordination, but there was no uniformity of penalty or enforcement. Discipline in the partisan ranks was much looser than in the regular army, varying greatly from unit to unit, depending most of all on the personality of the commanding officer and the political officer.

Among the partisans, a less serious, but more common offense was sleeping while on guard duty. Sooner or later every partisan unit had to deal with this infraction. In some rare instances, offenders were actually shot. I remember hearing about two Jewish partisans—in separate and unrelated instances—who had been caught sleeping at their posts while on guard duty and who were then court-martialed and shot. Both offenders were new recruits, so their entire partisan careers lasted only a couple of months. Of course it is possible that the leadership in their units was interested in making an example of them and enforcing strict discipline "to encourage the others," and that possibly the outcome would have been the same had two non-Jewish sentries been caught in similar circumstances—I have no personal knowledge of either the men or their units. Nonetheless, the way the story was repeated at the time, it had a definite anti-Semitic twist to it. And it was my own experience that until a Jewish partisan proved himself, he was more tolerated than accepted. Right after I joined up, I was advised—or should I say warned?—by a couple of Jewish partisans who were old-timers that I must be especially careful on guard duty to adhere scrupulously and literally to the regulations. Failure to do so, they told me, could have quite dire consequences.

In our company, officers and men interacted in a comradely way, so severe punishment was not likely for the two men who refused to obey their platoon leader. Still, the possibility existed. In any case, the two obviously considered that the immediate danger of returning down along the log fence far outweighed the theoretical danger of punishment for insubordination.

This put the platoon leader in a bind. He was new to his assignment, having been called to head the platoon just before this operation when our regular platoon leader fell ill. Maybe this man was just wrong for the job, or maybe he didn't have a strong enough personality to inspire the obedience that military operations require. He knew that somehow, some way, the fallen executive officer had to be retrieved. His eyes wandered from face to face. He was obviously worried about being disobeyed a third time. His gaze fell on me, moved on, and then, a second later, returned. He was staring at me. I knew he was going to order me to go and retrieve our fallen commander. I also knew I would be unable to refuse his direct order, as the other two had. Then I heard myself say, "I volunteer."

I could see the look of relief spread over his face. The rest of the platoon breathed a little easier too, now that they were off the hook. My own thought was, "Well, now you've gone and done it. No turning back now." Actually, I had already figured out how to go about the retrieval properly. Judging by where I was when the machine gun fire hit, the exec, at the head of our line, must have been at or close to the far end of the log fence. I disregarded everybody else's fear about exploding rounds coming from inside the burning school and started out, upright and at a run, down the side of the fence next to the building.

I reached the far end of the fence. Now came the hard part. I cautiously peered around the end of the fence and, just as I expected, there was the executive officer, about two meters away from me. His body was in a sitting position, his back against the fence. His mouth was open as if he were trying to say something. Well, at least he's wounded, not dead, I thought. A dead man wouldn't be sitting up like that.

Before committing myself to the outside of the fence, I took a good look at the bunker in the distance. Then, hugging the ground, I slithered over to where the man was. His hands were on the submachine gun in his lap, as if ready to shoot. He didn't even look wounded, just resting. I gave him a tug and said his name in a whisper. No response. I said his name again. Still no response. And then I realized that he was dead.

I eased the body over and down to the ground, face up, and began pulling and dragging it back around the end of the log fence, the way I'd come. The two meters along the outside of the fence were the hardest. I didn't dare raise my head or body very high off the ground. It wasn't easy. The man was tall, solidly built, and probably weighed about ninety kilos.

I knew the worst was over when I finally maneuvered the body around to the inside of the fence, next to the burning building. I turned him over on his stomach and for the first time saw an exit wound at the back of the neck. The bullet that killed him had entered through his open mouth and then severed the spinal cord. Ammunition was still exploding inside the building but I really didn't pay much attention to it. It seemed pretty harmless. With only one pause to catch my breath, I dragged the body back to the other end of the fence and there the other partisans took it from me.

Without proper leadership, our sector was stalled. We milled about aimlessly, not knowing how or whether to continue. And then a large contingent from company two of the brigade arrived to give us a hand in silencing the German bunker. They reported that, except at the police station, resistance all over town was at an end. We could hear the chatter of machine gun and rifle fire coming from the direction of the police station, interrupted from time to time by the detonation of hand grenades.

The new men lined up at least a dozen machine guns and several mortars and directed a continuous stream of fire at the bunker, which responded in kind. I watched the tracer bullets with fascination. Every third or fourth round was a tracer to make it possible to aim at night. After about five minutes of this fire, the men in the bunker tried to escape toward the open fields behind. We cut down four of them as they emerged and found two more dead bodies just inside. All at once a deafening explosion shook the ground beneath us and then there was silence, both where we were and in town.

We later learned that the police station, the last and most stubbornly defended stronghold, had been brought down with heavy charges of *tol*. This was the tallest building in town. It stood three stories high and was of masonry construction. The chief of police and a few others had barricaded themselves on the top floor and were spraying anything that moved in the street below with machine gun fire. The partisans brought explosives into the ground floor. When the explosives went off, the building collapsed in on itself and the police defending it were buried in the rubble.

One of several other strongholds taken was the library, a one-story brick building, and all the enemy resisters it harbored were killed. One partisan from my platoon was also killed accidentally, by his own hand, when the library was taken. Back at base, this man was known for carrying around an anti-tank grenade clipped to his belt, even though the thing was heavy and bulky. During the attack on the library, the man used up his supply of regular hand grenades and then threw his faithful anti-tank grenade at one of the library windows, forgetting what he knew perfectly well, that this kind of grenade explodes on contact, which it did when it touched the glass in the window. The enormous explosion brought one whole side of the library down on top of the man, and he died instantly.

All told, eighty-seven policemen were killed during the course of our attack. Twenty-four more were taken captive and, after a day or two of interrogation, executed. As Soviet citizens, they were considered traitors to their country. Some pleaded with us to let them join our ranks, but their requests were judged more expedient than sincere and so were rejected out of hand. Locals who collaborated with the Germans were always the object of intense hatred and they were, as a rule, eliminated if captured. Those who came over to us of their own free will often brought with them weapons and important information and were usually accepted, after being subjected to suitable interrogation and tests of reliability and sincerity.

By contrast, Germans taken prisoner were not ordinarily executed, unless there was information specifically incriminating them in atrocities or other acts of cruelty against the partisans or the general population. During the year and a half I was an active partisan, I must have come across fifteen or so captured Germans, quietly living in partisan-controlled villages and working at their civilian trades, mostly as shoemakers or tailors.

The police never tried to come back into the town after we withdrew. For a long time it stood in no-man's-land, occupied by neither side. In the end, a partisan detachment was stationed there.

Our victory was costly, especially to my platoon, which lost five men that night. Of the thirty-five who went into the fight, only thirty returned alive. Casualty figures in the other companies were proportionately much smaller but still substantial—though in military terms acceptable. The enemy force, after all, had been annihilated.

A few days later I was ordered to report to company headquarters. There I found not only the commanding officer, but the company political officer and my platoon leader. They congratulated me for volunteering to retrieve the exec's body, and commended me for bravery in battle above and beyond the call of duty. For this, I was told, my name was being put in for a medal. I knew something like that took a very long time to go through and after a while I forgot all about it. Then, after the war, I left Russia and came to settle in the West. Many years afterwards, I was told by Shimon Zimmerman—who had stayed on in Russia longer than I did and who now lives in Israel—that he had seen, in a Russian newspaper, an official list of partisans who had received medals and that my name was on that list. And that's how I found out that I had been awarded the Red Star medal (*Orden krasnoj zvezdi*).

The two men who had disobeyed the direct order of their platoon leader were never called upon to account for what they had done. It is my understanding that our platoon leader didn't even report it. I can certainly believe he thought it reflected as much on him as on them and was quite content to keep the whole unfortunate incident out of the official records so that it would eventually be forgotten.

Our most important instrument for eating was the spoon. Not the fork, not the knife, but the ordinary, everyday spoon. We could easily get by without regular forks by using our "natural forks," as we used to call our fingers.

Knives weren't necessary because anything that needed cutting had been cut before it went into the cooking pot, and that included meat—when there was any. But without a spoon, there was no way you could eat soup, and soup, in one form or another, was the mainstay of our diet. Without a spoon you could literally go hungry.

Cabbage soup was a great favorite of ours and we had it often. Pumpkin soup was also popular, for an evening meal. Soup was eaten with quantities of bread. The bread would be cut or broken into chunks and the chunks placed on the table. We all ate from one large wooden soup bowl that sat in the middle of the table. You reached over, put your spoon in, and took what you wanted when you wanted it. This eating style was not because small, individual-sized bowls were lacking in a household, it was just the way people ate in the villages I visited.

Like the bowls, the spoons that the peasants and villagers used were usually made out of wood, too. Metal spoons made out of aluminum existed and were prized by the partisans because they were so much lighter and much less bulky than ordinary wooden spoons. You carried your metal spoon stuck in your boot and left the bowl sticking out. This habit was so common that people came to identify a partisan as much by his metal spoon as by the weapons he might be carrying. A few lucky souls proudly sported a combination spoon and fork that was Red Army issue. It was made of aluminum too and the fork end folded neatly back over the spoon.

Partisan spoons were rarely washed. When the meal was over, you thoughtfully licked your spoon clean and then tucked it back into your footgear.

In late October 1943, we prepared for a major offensive against the enemy, and the target picked was Lepel, a city of about twenty-five thousand inhabitants before the war, located forty kilometers or so south of our brigade base.

Lepel was well fortified. Large contingents of Germans and police were based there, and the city was surrounded by a network of seven small garrisons which would have to be dealt with before the city itself could be approached. Some 4000 *boitsi* (fighters), from five different brigades, were assembled for the assault. My entire Utkin brigade was included, as was the Melnikov brigade and two companies from the Dubrovtsi brigade. The latter brought along an artillery gun, but its aiming mechanism was faulty and it had to be aimed by sighting along the barrel.

To reach the designated assembly area we had to ford a river about a dozen meters across. The river was supposed to be shallow at the crossing point, no more than a foot or so deep, but perhaps the water had risen unexpectedly or the wrong site was chosen for the crossing. In fact, the water at the river crossing came up to a man's chest. We were obliged to undress and wade across the icy cold river holding our clothes and our rifles above our heads.

The assault on the garrisons around Lepel began with a night attack on two of them. After only an hour of fighting, resistance collapsed. The men at the remaining five garrisons fled into the city before we could get to them. Added to the enemy force already within the city, this meant that numerically the forces defending and attacking the city were approximately equal.

With the approaches to the city cleared, the main partisan offensive began. For three successive nights the city was attacked from all sides. During the daytime German planes circled constantly overhead, presumably photographing our numbers and locations. The first night of the attack my company was held in reserve. The second night we guarded the general staff headquarters, which bustled with activity as runners came and went to and from the front line. Some partisan units reached the center of the city that night, but could not overcome the resistance at certain strongholds, and so pulled back when dawn came.

In general, that was the tactic we employed. We were not strong enough to remain inside the city during the daylight hours. Consequently, what was conquered at night had to be given up when daylight came, and each night the attack began again from square one.

The third night, my company was part of the attacking force. We broke into the outskirts of the city easily enough but were pinned down trying to cross an open space further inside. The bullets seemed to come straight at us as we hugged the ground. It was sobering to see all those tracer bullets, like flies on a hot summer day, just above our heads. The ground was soggy and puddles an inch or two deep lay here and there. We were soon cold and wet, and we discovered we couldn't move forwards or backwards, because the main fire was coming from in front of us and was concentrated on an area just behind us. The enemy also kept up a steady barrage of mortar fire on the area just behind us, and we could hear the distinctive whoosh of the shells as they passed just above our heads. After what seemed an eternity, but was in fact no more than two hours, the enemy fire slackened off and we were able to pull back behind a building, there to await further orders.

The other units around the city were apparently faring no better than we were. The order came to withdraw. Our leadership was apparently convinced now that the city of Lepel was too big a morsel for us to swallow. We disbanded and returned to our bases.

Toward the end of 1943 the partisans planned a colossal, one-night attack on the railroads that was to cover a stretch of track close to two thousand kilometers in length. Night traffic had already been halted in many areas, but German countermeasures against attacks on the trains had been rather successful. As a result, it had now become quite difficult to derail the trains. At night, however, the tracks were still vulnerable, and for some time partisans had been going after the tracks in sorties usually undertaken by units of squad size, rarely as large as a full platoon. A little ball of *tol* placed at the neck of a rail could blow a hole in it, or crack and bend it, or at least weaken it enough to oblige the Germans to replace it. But the Germans had a good supply of track replacement in reserve and usually made repairs promptly.

Therefore, German rail traffic was being delayed rather than halted. The new partisan attack was planned to damage more track than the Germans could replace from reserves at hand, hopefully about two thousand kilometers of rail. The Germans would have to send to the west for replacements, thus tying their lines up even further. The partisan attack was also planned to coincide with a big Red Army offensive to the east. A break in the supply line to the German armies at the front at this particular time could prove to be of paramount importance to the success of the offensive.

The targeted stretch of track ran from the city of Velikie Luki, in the north and near the front, down into the Ukraine, in the south. On the day of the operation, the partisan platoons were assembled separately, the plan of attack explained, and the attack itself rehearsed. Each of us was given two balls of *tol* with fuses and fifty-centimeter lengths of detonator cord. When the platoon got to the roadbed, we were to spread out until we were about six meters apart. We were to place the *tol* at the neck of the rail, attach and then light the cord, and get out. It sounded simple enough.

But matches were in short supply and cigarette lighters non-existent. How to light the pieces of cord that led to the fuses? The problem was solved by giving us lengths of nylon rope which, when lighted, burned slowly and glowed, much like a cigarette. Unlike a cigarette, the nylon rope didn't stop burning until it was completely burned up.

We dispersed to rest up for the night operation. The

more I thought about it, the more I came to have doubts. I could see a technical deficiency in the plan. It would be impossible for the little explosions all to go off at the same time. So the first explosion in a sector would have a tendency to jar nearby cakes of *tol* off the rail and onto the ground where they would explode more or less harmlessly. Something was needed to make the *tol* stick to the rail and anchor it there.

Then I remembered I had seen a ball of rusty wire somewhere in the village. After a short search I located it and broke off a length to experiment with. Within minutes I had fashioned a contraption one end of which gripped the rail from the top, while the other end kept the *tol* tight against the rail.

I rushed to my commanding officer, explained the problem to him, and showed him my solution. His face broke out in a grin from ear to ear. "Well done," he said. "Leave this here with me. I'll have everybody copy it."

The operation that night went off smoothly and I had the added satisfaction of knowing that all the explosives set off by my company had accomplished the maximum damage planned. Except for repair crews, there was no traffic on this railroad line for a full two weeks. Quite possibly other railroad lines were similarly attacked on that night. In any case, the operation was considered one of the most successful carried out by partisans and it no doubt had the desired impact on the Russian offensive that began shortly thereafter.

In the course of the winter of 1943–1944 we kept up our operations against the railroads and managed to derail two more trains further to the west. Closer to home, we often mined a section of heavily traveled highway between Lepel and the town of Kamen, and over a span of several months we managed to blow up a number of trucks. The Germans countered by covering fifteen kilometers of the highway with two parallel lengths of planking, fifty or sixty centimeters wide, which made mining the road next to impossible. The Germans also began to organize their trucks into large, protected convoys. Against these, ambushes were costly and impractical.

9

Another winter was coming to an end. Another spring was not far off. Our morale was high as news of more and more German defeats reached us. The Red Army forged ahead, piling victory upon victory as they moved steadily closer to us. Even though the front line was still far to the east, we could now contemplate the day when the Germans would be retreating through our area. Evidently the Germans also gave some thought to that eventuality. With so many partisans at their rear, they faced the real possibility of a coordinated partisan and Red Army attack.

The Germans assembled seven divisions of their own and, together with sizable units of the police, they prepared a systematic assault on the whole Ushachi county area occupied by the partisans. This area, which was about a hundred by forty kilometers in size, contained as many as 60,000 partisans. They had wrested it from German rule, village by village, and then had held off the Germans for over two years.

There were continual skirmishes along the perimeter. The fighting was on a relatively small scale, though, more or less one sector at a time. This time, however, the German assault, when it came, was mounted simultaneously from every side. Every sector was engaged. The enemy was determined to retake the territory and to wipe out the partisans once and for all. My company was sent to the front line, with the others, and given a sector to defend.

It was an unequal fight. The enemy forces far exceeded our own, both in numbers of men and in the quantity and quality of their equipment. It was estimated that some one hundred thousand Germans and police took part in the "blockade," as it was called. They made abundant use of tanks and artillery and sent planes to bombard and reconnoiter, whereas we were pretty much limited to small arms.

Yet for the first two weeks our resistance was strong. We clung to every hill and village and gave up very little territory. During daylight hours we were often bombarded by artillery and heavy mortar fire—and twice by planes— and we had to give up positions. But at night we usually counterattacked and regained the ground lost during the day. So far the casualties in my company were light, only one killed and a number wounded slightly.

Then the stress of unrelenting pressure began to take its toll. Lack of sleep and irregular and inadequate meals left us haggard and worn out, and there was no relief in sight. The few reserves the partisans had were needed in sectors more severely pressed than our own.

Our company entered a village late one afternoon. It was deserted. We hadn't eaten all day, so we scrounged around for food. Little was to be found until somebody discovered a few chickens loose in a yard. None of them got away and we ate well that night. We stayed overnight and breakfasted on leftovers.

Then the order came to move out. No sooner were we clear of the village when it came under a well-aimed heavy artillery bombardment. The first shell hit the house I had spent the night in. Other houses took direct hits too and were turned into shattered wood and rubble. By the time we got to our new position on a hill overlooking the village, about a kilometer away, hardly a house was left standing. I was not sure to what we owed our good fortune in getting out of the village in the nick of time—to the superior leadership of our officers, or to pure luck.

We settled down on the crest of the hill in trenches that had been dug months earlier with an eye to just such a need. The enemy apparently noticed activity on the hill and we started taking 88-millimeter mortar fire. After a while, it slowed down to a round every five or ten minutes, as if to let us know we hadn't been forgotten. Luckily for us, the rounds kept landing on the opposite end of the crest from where we were. But the enemy did not follow up with an advance on our position. We stayed put for most of the day, without food or water, and got the order to come down late in the afternoon. We felt disheartened. Our morale was definitely suffering from the frequent German bombardments and lack of sleep. A good part of every night was spent either in fighting or on guard duty. We were going into our third straight week of combat.

A rumor spread among us that Russian planes were going to fly in at midnight and strike the enemy positions facing us. At first I thought it was just wishful thinking, but when preparations began for the signal to the pilots I knew it was for real. The signal consisted of large piles of dry branches set out in the shape of the letter "T," taken as an arrow pointing to the strike area a quarter of a kilometer away. As soon as the planes could be heard coming, the dry branches would be set on fire.

We were excited by the prospect of the enemy getting a taste of the same medicine we'd been forced to swallow for two weeks. And then I began to wonder how effective such a bombardment could be if all the pilots had to go on was a burning "T" on the ground. The chief benefit would likely be only psychological.

I came off guard duty an hour or so before midnight and

settled in for the rest of the night in an isolated house we were using. I was roused from deep sleep by the sound of explosions not too far away. It took me a moment to wake up enough to realize what was going on. When I did, I overcame my fatigue and my reluctance to leave the spot on the floor where I was comfortably stretched out, and went outside where other partisans had already gathered to watch the spectacle. The bombing pattern, which lasted five to seven minutes, suggested that two or three planes were taking part in it. It was like music to our ears, a beautiful sight to behold.

In the morning, we pulled back to new positions. The Germans had broken through in a neighboring sector and this left us exposed. The situation was visibly deteriorating, yet so far my company had been lucky enough not to suffer any additional casualties. The enemy attacks continued without letup, and we were forced to give up more and more ground, which our nighttime counteroffensives could not regain.

Our last attempt to retake a village came in the fifth week of fighting. My company had gathered at night at the edge of a forest. The brigade political officer himself (*komissar brigady*) arrived before the attack to give us a pep talk. He was an imposing-looking man, middle-aged, and before the war he had been an important party official. He spoke at length—quite eloquently—and concluded by telling us one last time how important it was to retake the village. He was trying to whip up a little enthusiasm where there was none. He exhorted us to be prepared to sacrifice ourselves "for motherland and for Stalin (*za rodinu i za Stalina*)."

We had already spent a full day in the trenches, fighting off two frontal attacks by a German unit of company size. Each time our stiff resistance forced the Germans to retreat, we took a shelling from their artillery and heavy mortars. On the third attack we could resist no longer and fell back, and the village fell to the enemy.

By the time the political officer spoke, there wasn't much fight left in us. We were silently convinced that, given the superior weapons the enemy had used against us during the day, we weren't going to wrest the village from them that night. Consequently, our midnight attack was half-hearted, and we pulled back as soon as the enemy discovered us and opened up with a barrage of fire. That night, at least, none of us was ready to die, not even for Stalin!

There wasn't much fighting taking place to our west. The main German push was apparently coming from the north and from the east and it was driving us westward. By the middle of the fifth week of fighting, the area of partisan-controlled land had shrunk to about twenty by ten kilometers in size and was still shrinking.

During a lull in the fighting in our sector, I asked and received permission to go see the shoemaker at our brigade base village, about ten kilometers away and still under partisan control. My boots were literally falling apart. Only string was holding them together. Earlier, I had left some leather with the shoemaker, and I was anxious to pick up the new pair of boots while the village was still in partisan hands.

On my way to fetch the new boots I stopped off at the village where my old bookkeeping teacher lived. To my surprise, I found that about thirty Jews had gathered there with him—about half of all the Jews then living in Ushachi county. I had met some of them before, when I was traveling through the villages of our area. They had been forced to flee before the German advance and had congregated together as people who are threatened will do, to derive solace and support from each other. I could see they felt trapped and bewildered by what was happening and looked to me for encouraging news. Alas, I had none to give them. The situation was grim. We couldn't hold on much longer, a week or two at most, I thought. I described to them the situation as I saw it and tried not to sound too alarmist, but I told them that staying together like this, in one village, was not a good idea. (I privately considered it the worst thing they could do.) Separated, each one near a partisan unit or with local acquaintances, their chances would be much better. And with that, I wished them well and continued on my way. I still had a lot of territory to cover before nightfall.

A couple of kilometers futher on I met Artsik Gotyes (Dinerstein), from my hometown of Kurenits, going in the opposite direction and driving a horse and wagon loaded with food for a partisan unit. We stopped and talked for five minutes or so and then went on our separate ways. He, at least, was attached to a partisan unit, as a teamster, and his chances of survival would be much better than the large group of Jews I had just left. The net thrown by the Germans around all of us was getting tighter by the day and would soon close altogether. I had probably seen them for the last time and there was absolutely nothing I could do for them. We partisans were, of course, also vulnerable, to a lesser degree, perhaps, but still vulnerable. We had the option of fighting our way out. But at what cost?

Instead of holding out for two more weeks, our defense posture collapsed only two days later. The net closed and all the Jews I had seen that day, including Artsik Gotyes, perished, as did all but a handful of the others living in Ushachi county. Civilians attached to a partisan unit got no special protection at all when things fell apart. The partisans were too busy fighting for their own survival and completely overlooked the special vulnerability of the Jews.

One of the families left to fend for themselves were the Narotskys, originally from the town of Myadel, about thirty-five kilometers from Kurenits. The mother and a couple of the children had been killed during the German "action" in their town, but the father and a daughter named Leyka had escaped. He was an expert in leather goods and offered his services to the partisans, who gladly accepted. He then worked for them for a year and a half, turning horsehides and cowhides into good leather for different kinds of footwear. He was, in fact, the person who had given me leather for new boots when I visited him and his daughter before the blockade began. The partisans appreciated the excellent work he did for them, but when the crunch came, father and daughter were abandoned. The father struck me as a man of strong will. He knew that to be found alive with his daughter would automatically condemn her. Without him her chances would improve. He committed suicide by drowning after advising his daughter to pass herself off as a Tatar woman. She watched him wade into a lake, going deeper and deeper and then saw the water close in over him as he disappeared from her sight. Leyka told me every detail of the story when I met her again shortly after the liberation.

I was still heading to our base village to pick up my new boots. When I got there, after an absence of five weeks, it looked strangely quiet and half-deserted. But the shoemaker was still at home, working away. My boots? No, he hadn't got around to working on them yet. Maybe he'd be able to get started in a couple of days or a week, he said. I had the feeling he'd just as soon not work on partisan footwear anymore, now that our fortunes were failing. His metamorphosis from partisan member to peasant villager had already taken place.

So, nothing was left for me to do but return to my unit at the front line empty-handed. I took a long look at the shoemaker, his house, and the village, and felt it would be the last time I would see them. At nightfall, when I rejoined my comrades at the perimeter, they were right where I'd left them. It had been a quiet day at the front.

The next day the order came to abandon all our positions after sundown, and to do it as quietly as possible so as not to give the enemy any inkling of what was taking place. According to one rumor circulating, all partisans were withdrawing en masse to one designated area. There a decision would be made about the best way of breaking out of the encirclement. The general staff, which had been directing the defense of the whole Ushachi area, had decided that continued front-line resistance was counterproductive and could well lead to a total collapse and possible annihilation. Survival called for a concentrated breakout as soon as possible.

We started off and marched all night, and the closer we came to the designated area, the more partisan units we encountered. Thousands of partisans were streaming in from all directions to a central area about four by three kilometers in size. Some brigades I recognized. Others had names I'd never even heard before. The country roads leading in were primitive and narrow, and could accommodate horse and wagon traffic going one direction only. These dirt lanes went mainly through woods, with clearings only here and there.

My company was traveling light. Just one horse and wagon carried all our supplies. Other companies and brigades were coming in with many horse-and-wagon teams, which carried heavy weapons and ammunition in addition to food and supplies. So many vehicles converging on one small area resulted, inevitably, in congestion that stopped traffic as far as three or four kilometers from the designated assembly area. I saw four cannons pulled by a team of beautiful horses that had come to a complete halt because an overturned wagon blocked their way. Only people on foot could get around and through. Those cannons must have been the famous Dubrovtsi brigade artillery.

Traffic was tied up wherever two roads intersected. At this stage of the retreat every unit was still trying to bring with them everything they had—arms, equipment, food, and other supplies. Within twenty-four hours, all the horses and wagons would be abandoned. Anything that the men couldn't carry themselves was left behind, including the Dubrovtsi guns.

By morning we had settled down in the woods by the edge of a large clearing. The brigade commanders were supposedly meeting somewhere in the vicinity to decide on the next move. The question, so we were told, was whether to make a concerted breakout effort together, or to let each brigade do as best it could on its own.

By the middle of the morning, the rumor went around that it had been decided to let each brigade act independently. We heard that the Russian lieutenant-general who headed the whole Ushachi county partisan force had been whisked out by a small plane sent in for him during the night. That piece of news disturbed me more than any of the others at the time because it suggested impending disaster.

Around noon, half a dozen or so enemy planes subjected us to a lengthy aerial bombardment. There were casualties, but none in my brigade. When the bombing stopped, movement in the clearing picked up again. People were making final preparations for the coming night, when breakouts would be attempted.

Crossing the clearing on my way to a water source, I suddenly came face to face with Shimon Alperovits, a fellow native of Kurenits and a member of my old company. Shimon was about ten years my senior and an intelligent man from a fine family. For the past two months he'd been assigned to brigade headquarters as a German interpreter. We stopped and talked awhile. There wasn't much encouragement we could give each other. The situation was fluid and we both knew it was going to be a rough night ahead. Then we parted to go in opposite directions. That was the last time I saw Shimon; he was killed the next morning.

Later that afternoon my company moved to another location to get ready for the breakout attempt that night. Crossing the clearing, I saw two women coming towards us. As we got closer I was surprsied to see that it was the sisters Reykhe and Relke Alperovits (Naftolye's) from Kurenits. They explained that they had followed a partisan unit that had been stationed near their village because they knew some of the partisans in it. But here in the designated area they had been shooed away from that unit and no other's would have anything to do with them. They looked as forlorn as a pair of orphans.

I explained their plight to my platoon leader and added that they were relatives of mine, so could they join us? The platoon leader wasn't happy about it, but he reluctantly agreed. I took them over to my squad, saw that they had something to eat, and told them to stay close to me, come what may.

By sundown all the brigades were into the final stages of preparation. We heard that some had decided to break out back towards the east, where we had come from. Others, like my brigade, had decided to try and break out toward the west. The day before, we had been issued knapsacks made of white linen. These were to hold extra ammunition clips, a dry pair of leggings, and some food. They also had another purpose, just as important. Since the plan was for us to walk single-file through the woods at night, the white color of the knapsacks would help us see the person ahead better and so would minimize the chances of losing each other.

Just before we started out, my company commander took his horse a little ways into the darkening woods and shot him. He loved that horse and couldn't bear the thought that it might fall into German hands.

The sun had disappeared below the horizon. Twilight lingered in the treetops. We set out, about a thousand of us, in a single-file column. Then it was really dark, and the white of the knapsack of the person in front of me made it easier to follow as we made our way through trees and underbrush. Every so often I would glance back over my shoulder to check on the Alperovits sisters to make certain they were right behind me. We had orders to maintain strict silence, so talk was out of the question.

About an hour into the march, I noticed that a couple of partisans had come between me and the Alperovits sisters. Later, they were even further behind, and there was no way I could find out why.

Our column would sometimes slow down for no apparent reason and then continue at a quick run. After a while the reason for it became clear. When the man at the head of the column ran into an obstacle, like a pool of water or a fallen tree, he had to slow down in order to climb around it or over it, and the people behind him were in turn obliged to slacken their pace while he did so. But once the man had negotiated the obstacle, he went on again at the same speed as before, and the people behind him, after negotiating the obstacle in their turn, now had to run in order to catch up. This slowdown-speedup then worked its way back to the end of the column, getting more exaggerated as it did so.

By now the column must have stretched out over a distance of one and a half kilometers, and I was positioned perhaps a third of the way from the end. When the slowdowns reached me, they had turned into standing in place for as long as half a minute. Then, after I had gotten over or around whatever it was, I had to sprint so as not to lose the white speck in front of me that was disappearing around some undergrowth or tree. This kind of a march was new to all of us; that is, we had never trained for it. So the people toward the head of the column kept pressing forward, oblivious to the difficulties they were causing for those of us toward the end.

When you're climbing around or over something, you naturally lower your gaze and focus your attention on what you're doing—which means you can't simultaneously be watching the person in front, who has already started to run in order not to lose track of the person in front of him. When you do get over or around the obstacle and can raise your eyes again, you may have momentarily lost the person in front of you. You take a few quick steps first in one direction, then in another, and you still can't find the person. At this point the column has been broken, and now you and everyone behind you have been severed from those in front.

And this in fact was what happened. Not once, but three separate times. About three hours into the march I noticed there were only three people left immediately behind me. That meant that at least the trailing quarter of the column had broken away and in that trailing quarter were the two Alperovits sisters from Kurenits.

Getting severed from the column was not necessarily a disaster, provided that within the severed segment there was an officer of rank high enough to have been briefed as to where the full column was headed. The severed segment could then proceed on its own to the designated area. But a severed segment without such an officer was another story. For all practical purposes they were lost in a forest that during the next couple of days would be thoroughly searched by enemy forces.

The segment that broke off behind me did not have anybody in it who knew the location from which the break-out was going to be staged, or how to get there. I never found out just what happened to them. Many, I suppose, succeeded in breaking out or, if not, somehow avoiding detection. But others did not, and Reykhe and Relke were among them. They perished in the woods.

Since I was all too aware of the consequences of breaking the column, I was more careful than ever not to let the person in front of me get out of sight. But after another hour it became apparent that I too was part of a short trailing segment that had broken off from the main column. There were about thirty-five to forty of us, and we were truly leaderless, with no idea at all where we should be heading. We milled around for a bit, and then we sat down on the ground, dejected, and quietly cursed our bad luck. Up ahead I could see a small, treeless area covered with a light mist, a bog or maybe a ravine.

We must have sat where we were for well over an hour. I might well be facing Germans very soon, maybe within just a few hours. And as I sat brooding about my likely fate, I suddenly heard something like a faint rattle. The sound was coming from the area in front of us which was covered by the mist and was getting louder.

I now recognized it as the sound made by someone running with a light machine gun of the type with which our partisans were equipped. It had a round, flat bullet magazine in which the bullets would stack up somewhat loosely. When you ran with such a machine gun, the bullets would make a distinct rattling sound that we were all familiar with. Because of the fog, we couldn't see whoever it was but were sufficiently desperate to break the rule of silence. Somebody called out. After a couple of louder shouts, the man emerged from the fog and we learned that he was from a group of about two hundred and fifty—the middle of the column—that had also broken off and was trying to find the leading end of the column again. He sounded disappointed that we weren't what he was looking for. That was not our reaction, however. We were ecstatic, particularly when the segment turned out to be my old company, including the young lieutenant who was their commanding officer and who did know where we were going and how to get there.

This time we moved out at a pretty fast clip. Too much time had been lost, and before long dawn would dissipate our cover of darkness. In fact, by the time we got to the staging area for the breakout, the first light had already appeared in the sky. The front end of the column had got to the staging area ahead of us and was waiting for us to appear. We were way behind schedule. The original plan was for the breakout to take place at night. That advantage had now been lost.

We were stretched out along the edge of the forest, facing a large clearing perhaps a kilometer square. To the right of the clearing, we could make out some buildings and these, we were told, housed a strong enemy garrison. Off to the left, beyond where we could see, was another garrison. Straight ahead at the far side of the clearing, and also not yet visible, was a lake. Our escape route lay through a narrow neck of land between the lake and the still invisible garrison to the left. If we could make it through that neck of land, we could consider ourselves safe, at least for the moment.

It was already quite light by the time we were positioned properly to advance through the clearing. The sun hadn't come up yet, but it would any minute. This was obviously an operation that should have taken place at night. Getting across the clearing in broad daylight was going to be many times more hazardous, but there was nothing to be done about it now.

In a broad line, we stepped out of the forest and into the clearing. We moved slowly at first and then picked up the pace. There were about seven hundred of us. It felt like walking through a minefield. The way to freedom lay about a kilometer and a half away, diagonally to our left. I knew from past experience that those who took the lead in a maneuver like this usually stood a better chance of getting through than did those who fell behind. I desperately wanted to succeed in getting out. I moved forward as fast as I could under the circumstances. A glance back showed that many of the men had covered already about a quarter of the distance, but others were still close to the edge of the forest.

And then the first shots were heard. We had been discovered. There was machine gun fire from the garrison to our right, followed, before long, by mortars. I could hear bullets fly close by, and behind me I could hear the bursts of mortar rounds going off. There was no thought of stopping to counter with fire of our own. I bent forward and kept moving as fast as I could. Not far from me I noticed a young man from Kurenits, Zalman Alperovits (Maysyeys). He wasn't quite seventeen years old and belonged to company two of the brigade. I was glad to see him and urged him to stay close. For the next few minutes we did stay together, but then we lost each other in the general confusion of dodging the incoming fire and getting around elevated spots on the ground. When I realized he wasn't there anymore, my heart sank, not just because I felt protective of him because of his tender age, but also because together we could have looked out for each other in case one of us was wounded.

I was now running, bent over as far as I could. I held my rifle in my right hand. Suddenly I felt the rifle butt kick my leg just above the knee. I guessed what it was but could not verify it. It was dangerous to divert my eyes from the terrain in front of me. I believed a bullet had struck the rifle and I had been spared an incapacitating leg injury. If the angle of the rifle had been just slightly different—and I was changing it often just for comfort—I would have been lying on the ground and unable to move, a fate to be dreaded much more than instant death. I was flooded with the warm feeling of satisfaction you get when you hear very good news. A feeling of renewed confidence surged throughout me. I remember thinking, "Yes, I'm going to make it after all!"

And then there was the lake in front of me. I veered to the left and followed the shoreline. I was shocked to see how many bullets were hitting the water and making little geysers. It gave me an idea how heavy the machine gun fire really was. I could now see what they had called "the neck" we had to pass through. I glanced around once more and saw there were partisans spread out all over the clearing, some, inexplicably, far behind. I also took in that the ground was dotted with the fallen, some immobile, others moving slightly.

I was just coming out at the far end of the neck when the first burst of an artillery salvo landed behind me. I pushed myself to the limit of my endurance and dashed across to the other side. There I joined about eighty partisans who had already made it to safety before me. A barrage of artillery fire closed the neck behind us as effectively as if an impenetrable wall had been erected. Nobody else could get through.

We were standing on ground distinctly lower than the clearing and were, as I was about to discover, near a bog. But we were out of sight of the gunners and felt safe. That also meant we could not see beyond the exploding shells and had no idea what was going on on the other side.

A partisan walked over to me and said he'd seen one of my Jewish friends lying in the middle of the clearing, wounded in both legs and holding a grenade in his hand. He said he was going to blow himself up, rather than let the Germans take him alive. It would have to be one of the two other Jewish partisans in my company, both from the tiny town of Neyke, about eight or nine kilometers from Kurenits. He was never seen again, so he must have done what he said he would. He was a brave young man, and a fighter who always gave a good account of himself in every encounter with the enemy.

I now had a chance to examine my rifle for the first time since I thought it had stopped a bullet headed for my leg. It was just as I had surmised; the wooden stock was cracked and a chunk was missing where the bullet had impacted, before going on to knock the range finder off the barrel. I owed a lot to good luck and this rifle. It had saved my life.

I shuddered when I thought how close I had come to sharing the fate of the young man from Neyke.

We waited for another half hour or so and when nobody else came through the neck, we knew the game was up for the others. Those who could would return to the temporary safety of the forest. And after that? I imagined the worst, but luckily it didn't turn out that way.

After the liberation by the Red Army, about two months later, we went back to Ushachi county and I ran into Zalman again, safe and sound. I was as glad to see him as if he had been my own brother. He was still two weeks short of seventeen and was allowed those two weeks off before being officially mobilized into the Red Army. We spent a couple of days together and reminisced about the breakout. He said that more than eighty percent of those who managed to get back to forest cover survived, either by staying hidden or by outmaneuvering their pursuers. With us at this time were also Dr. Tsirinski and Rokhel Dimentstein, both from Kurenits. The partisans, who needed medical expertise, had taken Dr. Tsirinski from Kurenits in the summer of 1942, and he eventually became chief medical officer of my Utkin brigade. A total of eighty-five of us from my brigade actually succeeded in breaking out, including half from my company. Both the commanding officer and the political officer came through, but my old friend Kulik was killed in the clearing. My friend Vasil also came through safe and sound, but was separated from me during this ordeal.

Those of us who had made it through the neck started on again. We moved down towards the bog, which stretched ahead for several kilometers. Walking through it was an ordeal in itself. The water came up to our knees much of the time and the ground under our feet moved up and down. The surface was sprinkled with wild cranberries, the remnant of the last year's harvest. We picked all we could reach and ate them as we went. It took several hours to get through the relatively few kilometeres of bog, and when we came out on the far side, it felt good to have solid ground under our feet again. The area we came into was strangely uninhabited, as if very few humans had ever set foot there. In the few hours of marching before the sun set, we encountered no villages, not even an isolated house. The one wagon track we crossed looked little used.

We stopped for the night at a dry, wooded spot. The last forty-eight hours had taken its toll. We were tired and hungry. Somebody discovered a pit with potatoes in it, and in short order we had them boiling in a big metal water pail, also from the pit. But the meal didn't turn out as good as expected. We found the potatoes had a sickly sweet taste, the kind that frost damage gives. Nonetheless, we all ate because we were so hungry, but few of us were able to keep the potatoes down. Our sensitive stomachs revolted.

The next morning we ran into a stray cow, and in short order had consumed all of it, skewering chunks of meat on branches over a fire and even picking the bones clean.

We didn't come to a village until the third day. We were now in the West, in the area that had been part of Poland before 1939. There was no more urgency to keep going further west. It was comparatively safe to move around in broad daylight here, much as it had been in Ushachi county before the blockade. When we found a suitable village, we stopped for a few days and got the rest we so badly needed.

My old commander, as ranking officer, had taken command of our group, made up of men from several companies of our brigade. Other groups of partisans, from various brigades, also found refuge in this area, which was in the vicinity of the town of Disna. We had no communication, of course, with the rest of our brigade; in fact we didn't even know what had happened to them.

For the next three weeks we drifted from village to village, never staying longer than three or four days in any one place. We had no plan of action and we didn't undertake any initiative against the enemy as this was not an area we were familiar with. At most, small details of three to five men would be sent out into German-controlled territory to look for food.

Then, before we had fully recovered from the effects of the first blockade, my group and all the other units in this area were hit with another one. To surround this area was a much simpler task for the Germans than Ushachi county had been. There, the partisan area was many times larger. It also had a well-established defense perimeter, run and coordinated by a single high command. Partisans' resistance there could truly be described as fierce, especially in the first three weeks. Here, in the Disna region, there was no coordinated command, no established perimeter to defend, and hardly any resistance to the German challenge. The partisans here—relatively few in number—consisted of small bands of fighters, mostly remnants of once strong brigades, which were hardly in touch with each other. We were all still "licking our wounds" from the consequences of the first blockade. To top it off, this area was topographically more conducive to encirclement. It was within a triangle, two sides of which were formed by medium-size rivers and a lake, and the third by a two-lane modern highway.

Early one evening the Germans surrounded the entire area with a sufficient number of troops to effectively trap all the partisans within it.

By chance, I was outside the trap when it was sprung. That afternoon five of us had been sent out into German-controlled territory to scrounge up food on the far side of the two-lane highway. We had found a wagon and loaded it up with bread, grains, and other foodstuffs. Toward nightfall we were getting ready to cross the highway back into partisan territory when we heard German vehicles and saw helmeted troops silhouetted against the sky. Up to that time the highway, because of partisan activity, had been entirely devoid of traffic, so we immediately knew something was up. We moved back and approached the highway again a couple of kilometers away. Here too there were German troops. Only one explanation was possible—a blockade.

We abandoned the horse and wagon and moved back away from the highway. The moon was out and visibility was good. We were all set to open fire on three bobbing heads in a corn field when we recognized them as partisans in the same predicament as ourselves. They joined forces with us, and we kept moving back, away from the blockaded area.

We came to a creek about six meters across. There was a bridge seventy-five meters or so away and we followed the bank of the creek towards it. About halfway there, a machine gun positioned on the bridge or close by opened fire on us. Our only hope lay in getting to the cover of woods on the far side of the creek. The creek was too wide to jump, but we tried anyway and landed in the middle, where the water turned out to be only waist deep.

The shooting continued. Under fire we crawled across a potato field and finally reached the trees. Only then did the firing stop. The moon shone brightly in the cloudless sky. Luckily, none of us had been hit.

In my haste to get across the creek I had discarded the old sheepskin coat that had served me so well and faithfully for so long. Somehow I had managed to hold onto it all through the first blockade and the five weeks of fighting before that. Now, in a sudden decision, I dropped it at the edge of the creek, realizing that when soaked it would weigh me down intolerably. Within minutes, I regretted my impulsive decision. For several weeks I continued to miss it, like a child his security blanket. I missed its warmth in the still chilly nights, and during the day I missed its protection against mosquitoes.

As far as we knew, there were no forests of any size in this area, at least none large enough to give protection during the daylight hours, only small patches of woods. With dawn approaching, we selected a wooded plot about two acres in size. It was mostly young birches, but they were growing close together and we hoped that would provide us with acceptable cover.

We spent the whole day hunkered down in those birches. We heard peasants drive by with horse and wagon. We heard peasants walking and talking not very far away. If they had discovered us, they could very well have denounced us to the Germans. Luckily, we went undetected.

As we waited for night to come, we tried to come to some sort of decision about what to do next. The highest ranking man of our original group of five was a squad leader, one of the three partisans who had joined us was a platoon leader. His pregnant wife was trapped inside the triangle. He insisted on our crossing the highway so we could rejoin our units. As he was the senior person present, most of the others deferred to him for guidance and decision making. I, however, argued against crossing the highway into the trap. The units inside would eventually have to break out into the area where we now were. It would be foolish to subject ourselves to considerable danger twice, both crossing the highway into the trap and then crossing the highway again to break out. I proposed we find a place with better cover on this side of the road and wait for the others to join us. I suspected the platoon leader's concern for his wife was clouding his better judgment.

My own squad leader, who had no opinion of his own, and the others in my group, vacillated back and forth all day. In the end, the platoon leader prevailed. We would try and cross the highway that night. As much as I didn't like the decision, and thought it illogical, even foolhardy, I still felt I had to go along with it.

At dusk we left our cover, cautiously approached a couple of houses, and asked for something to eat. When our hunger was satisfied, we went from house to house until we found a peasant who looked trustworthy enough to act as a guide for us. He and two others of our group went out to reconnoiter the highway. They returned to report that there were still many Germans there and that trying to get across just then would be too hazardous.

At dawn we selected a large marshy area and there we spent the day. It looked rather uninviting, but that was what we wanted. For security we needed a spot that local people would not be wandering into for wood, or mushrooms, or berries, as they might with a drier location. But we paid a price for the extra measure of security. It turned out to be an oppressively hot and steamy summer's day when everything hung limp. Giant mosquitoes tormented us. Every exposed part of my body was savaged. And we dared not build a fire for smoke protection. We were glad to see the sun go down so we could leave the place.

We collected food again in the evening and picked another guide, this time a man about fifty, who had a strange way of acting. Every thirty meters or so he would stop, bend down or crouch as if expecting a sudden attack, and then he would sweep the terrain with his eyes for a full minute before straightening up and moving forward again, only to repeat the whole business all over again a short distance further on. He was a poor choice for a guide. I thought that at this pace, it would be dawn before we reached the highway. I was wrong. We did reach the highway before dawn, though much later than we had intended.

We dismissed the strange man within sight of the highway, reconnoitered, and promptly came upon a detail of Germans waiting in ambush along the highway. We discovered them by the glow of the cigarettes they were smoking. They must have gotten careless because they weren't expecting partisans from our side of the road.

We moved a hundred meters away, parallel to the road, and were getting set to make our dash across it when we heard shooting break out in the distance—perhaps two or three kilometers further down the highway. This would surely be a breakout attempt by the encircled partisans. Machine guns joined the fray and then we heard the sound of exploding mortar rounds. The battle lasted at full fury for twenty or twenty-five minutes. No small-scale breakout, we agreed. Two days later we learned that in fact fully eighty to ninety percent of all units inside the triangle came across the highway that evening. When challenged, they fought their way out, broke through the German positions, and dispersed the enemy. In my own mind, I had never doubted the partisans' ability to accomplish this and I fully expected there would be a breakout.

As we sat on the ground in a small wooded plot, about twenty meters from the highway, and listened to the sounds of battle dying out, we felt proud of our fellow partisans and happy that they had made it out of the encirclement, which we were confident they had done. We were also glad that fate had intervened in the person of our slow guide and so had kept us on this side of the highway.

We now started moving back away from the highway and by the first light of dawn, we were several kilometers away from it, but in the same general area where we had spent the last two days. We were looking for a clump of woods in which to hole up for the day again, when a young man emerged from nowhere and cut across our trail. Now that he had seen us, we couldn't really let him go, because he might betray us. He said he lived just a short half-kilometer away and was on his way home after spending the night with his girlfriend. We accompanied him the rest of the way to the isolated house where he lived. His parents, a middle-aged couple, gave us food but begged us not to stay in the house during the day. It wasn't safe, they said. German soldiers had come by the day before and they might do so again. They pointed to a tiny steambath house about 150 meters away and said it would be much safer for us to spend the day there. It had just started to rain, so we took their suggestion. We also took the son along as a hostage.

The bathhouse really was small. The inside dimensions were no more than three by two meters. In one corner, across from the door, sat a pile of rocks in the shape of an igloo. To get the bathhouse ready for use, the rock pile would be heated by burning wood underneath. After the smoke that had built up was let out, by opening the door, the bathers would come in and sit down on wooden benches. They made steam by pouring water on the heated rocks. There was no soap then, so the accumulated dirt and grime were steamed and sweated away, aided by a bundle of fresh, leafy twigs. You would flail every part of your body with this switch of twigs and get just as clean as if you had used the best soap. Steambath houses in this region were usually situated within easy access of a body of water, like a spring, a creek, or a lake. In winter, some hardy souls would run out of the steambath and plunge into the icy water, a feat I never personally cared to emulate.

Steambaths served another useful, and in fact indispensable, purpose. They were the chief means of delousing, and lice, unfortunately, were our constant companions because of the lack of soap. The only sure way of getting the little parasites out of your underwear was to hang it on a rope line over the heated rock pile. Even better results were obtained by putting the underwear directly on the rock pile. You had to be careful, though, not to leave it there more than a few seconds at a time, lest it catch fire. Many a bather left the bathhouse with less underwear than he came in with.

We spent the whole day in the little bathhouse. No Germans came our way, though we did observe two of them, through the little window, walk towards the house. We were prepared to fight in case they decided to approach the bathhouse. We were told later the Germans came only to ask for fresh eggs.

When darkness fell we were invited back inside the house and this time we were given a sumptuous meal. The farmer had butchered a sheep during the day. As we came inside, the aroma of the well-prepared dinner permeated the house. Our host then broke out quantities of locally distilled alcohol (*samogonka*), without which no White Russian meal is complete. It was an outstanding feast and no doubt the farmer's way of expressing his gratitude for leaving his son unharmed.

That night we continued marching away from the highway. By morning we had come into an area where we could apparently move around safely during the day as well. After an inquiry, we were directed to a village five kilometers distant, where partisans were said to have arrived. When we got there, we found almost our whole group. They had come through unscathed.

Our commanding officer was not among them, though. He had been ill with typhus when the Germans sealed off the triangle. When the company began its breakout, he was still weak and running a high temperature. He was carried by stretcher for a distance, until it became clear he probably would not survive the movement. He desperately needed rest. So it was decided to leave him there, with a squad of partisans and the company nurse, who was also his fiancée. They had enough food to last a week. By then, it was hoped, he would be sufficiently recovered to make it to the highway, with the squad of fighters.

A week later the squad leader appeared at our village with a tale of woe. He reported that all the others were dead. He alone had survived. For five days everything had been quiet in the marsh they had holed themselves up in. The commander was getting stronger every day. His fever left him. Although weak, he was starting to walk a little more each day. His confidence was returning with his strength. "Don't worry," he would say. "Another day or two and I'll have you all out of here." Then, on the fifth day, the Germans, who were systematically sweeping the area, discovered them. The partisans resisted bravely, but it was futile. The commander saw that all was lost. He took his revolver and shot his fiancée and then himself. Only the squad leader, who had hidden under branches and vegetation, escaped.

Our commander had been very well liked, and we all mourned his death and the death of the other ten of our comrades. The political officer took over effective command of our company. For several weeks we moved from village to village, and then orders came for us to return to the town of Ushachi.

The Ushachi region had already been liberated by the Red Army, while the area where we were was just then in the final throes of liberation. To keep out of the way of the Germans who were retreating from the Red Army, we kept to the back woods, away from the main highways, and even from smaller roads. We figured that the Germans, in their haste, would never use the back roads, some no more than wagon tracks.

Therefore we were shocked to see two German tanks suddenly appear in our midst. A German officer, exposed from the waist up in the lead tank, was frantically waving his arms as if to shoo us away and was screaming in German for us to get out of their way immediately. We froze where we stood, with confused and sheepish looks on our faces. There was no time. We couldn't fight. We couldn't run. We had absolutely nothing with which to stop a tank. I don't believe there was a tank grenade among us, and even if there had been, there wouldn't have been time to snatch it out of the bag and use it. There was no point in running. That would likely have provoked the tank gunners into making mincemeat of us. The same thing would have happened if somebody had shot the German officer, who made a very easy target.

And then, just as suddenly as they came, the tanks disappeared into the woods at the other side of the clearing. The whole business, from start to finish, had lasted no more than half a minute. The tanks had plowed through us like a ship through fog, neither one affected by the other. Some said that the tank crews had mistaken us for friendly civilians or collaborators, or even police. Others said the tank crews didn't care who we were. They just wanted to get away from the Red Army that was on their heels. We all felt we were a very lucky bunch of partisans to have come out of such an encounter with no more than our breath taken away. And as it turned out, this was the only encounter we had with the retreating German Wehrmacht.

We marched to the east all that day. In the afternoon we met the first unit of the Red Army coming in the opposite direction. It was a company of foot soldiers led by a captain riding a bicycle. He stopped to talk a minute, and the soldiers marched on past us. I was shocked by the appearance of our liberators; they looked so tired, so haggard, and so small. None looked over fifteen years old, though I knew they had to be at least seventeen before they could be drafted. I commented to the captain on their appearance. "Ah," he answered, "you should have seen those kids (*rebyata*) yesterday when they took hill number so-and-so from the Germans. They fought like heroes and they won." We talked for a while and then he got back on his bike and pedaled away to catch up with his men. We were the first partisans he had met. Apparently, he was as fascinated by us as we were in meeting the liberating Red Army.

Shortly thereafter, we met a large truck convoy heading west. Some of the trucks carried the famous Katyusha multiple-rocket launchers, sometimes called "Stalin organs." We'd heard how effective they were and how much the Germans feared them. Over the next few days we saw many of these Katyushas on their way to the front. They were always covered with a tarp, to keep the dust off no doubt, but also, we were told, to avoid displaying what they looked like. This weapon was considered one of the best the Red Army possessed and they were extremely proud of it.

Later in the afternoon we met other units of foot soldiers. One unit handed over to us a couple of policemen they had captured the day before and didn't know what to do with. One of the captured men was the head of the police station in a town nearby, and the other was his deputy. The townspeople had denounced them to this Red Army unit as it marched through their town. The partisans knew just how to deal with traitors like these. They were interrogated for ten to fifteen minutes, so that their identities and degree of collaboration with the enemy could be established, and then they were shot.

Our destination turned out not to be the town of Ushachi, but a village some distance from it. We pulled in a couple of days later, and there we found assembled just about the whole Utkin brigade, approximately ninety percent of the original force. About a hundred partisans had perished during the breakout and the five weeks of fighting that preceded it. I found most of the rest of my own company that had been forced to turn back during the breakout and I must say they looked none the worse for the experience.

We were told that the brigade was going to be disbanded the next day and simultaneously the men would be drafted into the Red Army. Out of the whole brigade only twenty-two partisans were exempted and I was one of them, thanks to the political officer (*komissar*) of my company. When the partisan leaders walked by me, standing in formation with the others, I heard the political officer say, "Let's leave this young man here. We'll need him to help build the county back up again. He has a good education and will make a fine teacher.'' I did not fully appreciate then that with those few words he had in effect saved my life.

Within six or seven weeks, few of the men from the Utkin brigade who were mobilized into the Red Army were still alive. They were all sent into battle without adequate preparation or any further training. Most fell in one particular offensive that took place in Prussia near the old city of Königsberg (today called Kaliningrad). Of the nine or ten Jewish men in the old Utkin brigade, I know of only one who survived, and he was badly wounded and had to spend six months in a hospital. In the spring of 1945 he came back to his hometown of Krivich. I was working there at the time and heard from him directly what had happened to our old friends and comrades. The man had been a tailor before the war and worked as one while he was with the partisans. Ironically, I don't think he ever carried a weapon or took part in any of our campaigns; I doubt if he even knew how to fire a rifle properly.

When the twenty-two of us who had been exempted from induction into the Red Army were discharged, we were each given a certificate attesting to our length of service with the Utkin brigade and describing our accomplishments. My certificate also noted that I'd been nominated for the Red Star medal. We were also permitted, for a while, to keep our weapons and to move around freely. Later I discovered the certificate was helpful in opening doors for better job opportunities.

I went to the town of Ushachi for a couple of days and there I met Zalman Alperovits again. He had been left behind for the two weeks until he would be seventeen years old, at which time he was to report for induction into the Red Army. He did so and somehow ended up with the other partisans from the old Utkin brigade. Unfortunately, he also shared their fate.

When I saw Zalman in Ushachi, I told him I planned to

go back to Kurenits. Six weeks later I got a letter from him saying he was with the army near Königsberg. He concluded with these words: "Tomorrow we all go into battle against the enemy—my first battle now that I'm a real soldier. If I survive, I'll write you." My heart skipped a beat as I read those words. The letter had taken seven or eight days to reach me, and at that moment I had a premonition that the writer of the letter was no longer alive. A month later his sister Rivka (Maysyeys) received official notification of his death in combat.

The idea for holding back our group of twenty-two had originally been to help in rebuilding the civil administration of Ushachi county. We soon learned, however, that this was an opportunity, not an obligation. Enough experienced personnel had arrived in the wake of the Red Army to take care of these functions quite adequately and more were arriving daily. We were welcome to stay, but we were free to leave.

Epilogue

Kurenits—Return
and Farewell

I decided to go back to Kurenits. Unlike some of the other survivors I met who were drawn to their hometowns because they harbored some hope of finding family and loved ones still alive there, I had no such illusions. For two years I had been quite aware of my own family's fate. Our beautiful big house was not what was in my mind. Without my parents and my sisters, the house meant absolutely nothing to me. It lost even its sentimental hold. What then was drawing me back to Kurenits? I think the answer can be found in an analogy with someone reading a book. He wants to know what happens in the last chapter before the book is returned to the shelf, not to be picked up again for many years or perhaps ever. The epilogue of the tragic story of Kurenits still had to be read. I was anxious to see what had happened to the town, even if it was just for the last time. I wanted to see its physical shape, to see the survivors who by now must have returned from the forest and whose final tally must be fewer than the time I last saw them in the Katlovtse forest. I wanted to see the place where my mother and my little nephew had been burned alive, along with so many other Jews, in the Kurenits "action." I wanted to see the pit where the "fifty-four" had been buried, where I could so easily have ended up myself. I had to see these things with different eyes, eyes devoid of fear, the eyes of a free man who had beaten the odds and who had survived.

So I left Ushachi and started back to Kurenits. I hitch-hiked and got rides with trucks, about the only means of transportation there was for civilians. My last ride dropped me off just a few kilometers outside of Kurenits. I walked the rest of the way, coming in on Myadler Street. I soon found that Eli Spektor and his family had taken up residence in one of the vacant Jewish houses there. Their old house, on the town square, had been burned down. They welcomed me and let me stay with them whenever I was in town. They brought me up to date on everything that had happened in the forest, and spoke of those who had survived and those who had not. In all, out of a Jewish population of about 2,000 in Kurenits before the Holocaust, only about 220 had survived.

I found the center of town destroyed. All but a couple of the houses on the square had burned down, including ours. This had been a farewell present from the local police just before they fled. They knew that some of the Kurenits Jews were still alive and out of their reach in the forest. To vent their frustration, they set fire to the buildings on the square, all of which were Jewish-owned.

Only the thick masonry walls of what had been our house remained standing. Strangely, this sight did not provoke any unhappiness in me. On the contrary, I felt relieved. It would make it easier for me to break with the town altogether. Had our house been spared its fate, and by a miracle left standing untouched, its use would have been denied me anyway. When the Soviets annexed eastern Poland in 1939, half of our house had been taken away from us. The city authorities had decided the house was too large for a family of five. Only twelve square meters of living space per person were allowed. The living room was converted to an office and a Russian family of four moved in with us. Under such rules, now that the rest of my family was gone, I would have been entitled to no more than one small room. In practical terms, the house the police destroyed belonged not to me but to the city. Now, looking at its ruins, even the emotional attachment had been severed.

Kurenits, where I had been born and raised, where I had first become aware of the world around me, and where I experienced love of family, no longer held any appeal for me. I felt I was a stranger in the town to which I was rooted by memories of warm love of family and where I experienced the joy of a happy childhood. This place, where I had first seen the beauty of the sky and where I had first smelled a flower—this place which, as a child, I had imagined to be the center of the world, now repelled me. Too many recent memories crowded in and dispelled the others.

I spent close to three weeks in Kurenits. I walked through every part of the town, as if searching for something. Maybe I was trying to understand why it had all happened. And yet I knew the question had no answer, certainly none that was to be found in the streets of Kurenits.

I knew a large number of the non-Jewish people in Kurenits and I had gone to school with their children. Interestingly enough, none of them, not one, approached me with any expression of sympathy or regret for what had taken place so recently. And these were the better people, the ones who had played no direct role in our tragedy and who, as far as I knew, had done nothing to help the Germans or the police.

Like the town square, all the synagogues had been burned; everything specifically Jewish had been destroyed. Jewish houses located on streets away from the square had been left untouched, perhaps for fear of setting fire to a whole neighborhood where Jewish and non-Jewish houses stood side by side.

I heard much, from the surviving Jews, of a righteous gentile by the name of Bakacz, who lived on Vileyka Street. He had managed to save a Torah scroll from one of the burning synagogues, exposing himself at the same time to reprisals from the police and to ridicule, or worse, from the bystanders. He guarded the scroll through the remainder of the occupation and handed it over to the first few Jews who returned to Kurenits. It was also said that he helped, as much as he could, with food and in other ways.

I went to pay a visit to this extraordinary man and to thank him for all he had done. I told him how grateful we all felt. He said he didn't feel he had done anything out of the ordinary. He said any decent human being would have done just what he did. True, I thought, true. He had only meant to express a sense of modesty and had managed in that one sentence to expose the cause of our predicament: "Any decent human being would have done what I did." How many more people like him were there, willing and ready to think and act like him? Unfortunately, too few.

In Ushachi I had run into some students from the medical school in the Russian city of Minsk. They had been third-year students when their education was interrupted at the beginning of the war. The school was now about to reopen and they were on their way back to resume their studies. I became friendly with two members of the group. They thought I already had enough schooling to get in and they urged me to apply for admission. I was now ready to give it a try. Education had always meant a great deal to me and my family, and the field of medicine especially appealed to me. I hitchhiked to Minsk and went to see the dean of admissions. I showed him the certificate I had received from the partisans and I could see he was impressed (which encouraged me to make the certificate a part of other official interviews). He talked with me at length about my education and then about my experiences as a partisan. I was pleasantly surprised when, at last, he told me I was accepted as a student for the coming school year. However, my medical career came to an end before I even had a chance to leave his office. As I got up to leave, the dean told me that, "by the way," he had assumed my partisan service exempted me from the draft. Only second-year students and those above were exempt on educational grounds. First-year students were not. With that information, my chances of becoming a doctor evaporated. It made no sense to start school only to be inducted into the army a short while thereafter.

And so I left Minsk. On the outskirts of town, trying to get a ride with a truck, I was stopped by a police patrol. My rifle had attracted their attention. I had been carrying it around with me ever since I had been discharged from the partisans. I had been stopped before and questioned about the rifle, but the partisan certificate had always proved adequate to explain things. This time it didn't work. The police completely ignored my explanation that the rifle had saved my life and that I was sentimentally attached to it. They said a new city ordinance had just gone into effect requiring civilians to give up any and all weapons in their possession. My rifle was confiscated on the spot. I felt as if I'd lost an old friend.

From Kurenits I often made the trip to Vileyka, the regional capital, to see what job opportunities there might be there, but without much success. I had definitely decided not to settle down in Kurenits. Finally, I landed a decent office job in the town of Krivich.

The present map of Poland does not resemble its prewar shape. Both the eastern and western borders have been moved a considerable distance to the west. Before 1939 Kurenits had belonged to Poland and had been located about sixty kilometers *west* of the Polish-Russian border;

now, in 1944, it was well inside the Soviet domain, some three hundred kilometers *east* of the new Polish-Russian border. With certain adjustments, the present Polish-Russian border is situated approximately where the Molotov-Ribbentrop agreement of 1939 established it. It is generally accepted that this agreement between Nazi Germany and the Soviet Union set the stage for the start of World War Two by making Hitler's eastern flank secure and so allowing Hitler to concentrate on the Western powers. After the war, by way of compensation for losing its eastern territories, Poland was allowed to annex an area of similar size from East Germany. Thus Poland retained approximately the same overall size it had had before 1939.

In 1945 the governments of Poland and the Soviet Union reached an agreement that allowed all persons who had been citizens of Poland before the war, but were now residing in Russia, to return to Poland if they so desired. For Jews, returning to Poland rarely indicated a desire to settle there. It was first and foremost a means of getting out of Russia and, after that, a springboard for emigration to Palestine or one of the Western countries, preferably outside of Europe. Just as I felt an aversion to staying in Kurenits, other Jewish survivors apparently were averse to staying in their hometowns and cities or even to remaining in Europe. In the years of 1945 and 1946, more than eighty percent of the Jewish survivors who could do so, chose to leave the Soviet Union, a country that up to that time had had hermetically sealed borders. These people left behind them homes and towns that could only be a constant reminder of the great tragedies that had befallen them. Only two Jews, both of them old men, chose to remain in Kurenits.

Kurenits, as I had known it when I was growing up, no longer existed. When I think of the Jewish life that once flourished in all those towns and shtetls of ours that so closely resembled each other and had such full community lives, my heart aches. It aches because that life and those Jews no longer exist. They have been obliterated and all trace of them has been erased from the places where they and their forefathers lived for centuries. All those Jewish communities have vanished from the face of the earth as surely and as permanently as has prehistoric man.

And so I too chose to leave the place of my birth and the land where my family and their families before had lived, a land that held memories of my early childhood. I spent the next three and a half years in a displaced persons camp in west Germany, until finally I came to the shores of the New World, and here I made a new life.

Index of Place Names

Index

894817